WITHDRAWN

SOUND
for the
STAGE
A Technical Handbook

Patrick M. Finelli

Drama Book Publishers
New York

Copyright © 1989 by Patrick Finelli

FIRST EDITION

All rights reserved under the International and Pan-American Copyright
Conventions. For information address Drama Book Publishers, 260 Fifth
Avenue, New York, New York 10001.

No part of this publication may be reproduced or transmitted in any form or by
any means, electronic or mechanical, including photocopy, recording, or any
information storage and retrieval system now known or to be invented, without
permission in writing from the publisher, except by a reviewer who wishes to
quote brief passages in connection with a review written for inclusion in a
magazine, newspaper or broadcast.

Library of Congress Cataloging-in-Publication Data

Finelli, Patrick M.
      Sound for the Stage: a technical handbook / Patrick M. Finelli.
          p. cm.
      Bibliography: p.
      Includes index.
      ISBN 0-89676-105-3 : $19.95
        1. Theaters—Electronic sound control.   I. Title.
TK7881.9.F36 1989
621.382'8—dc 19   89-1291
                                                           CIP

ISBN 0-89676-105-3

Manufactured in the United States of America

Acknowledgment

I wish to express sincere appreciation and gratitude to those people whose contributions made this book possible.

To my students at the University of South Florida

To my colleagues and staff in the Theatre Department

To Herb Schmoll and USF's College of Architecture

To Judith Holmes of Drama Books, for her diligent copy editing and work on the final manuscript

To Mark Katz, Susan Bean, Betty Lichtenberg and Lisa Conner, who helped review first drafts

To Patrick Gill, who used an early version of this text in his class at Cornell

To Bob Heil, for permission to use portions of his book listed in the bibliography

To Rollins Brook, for his inspirational USITT seminars and papers on microphones, loudspeakers and acoustics

To David Collison, for his pioneering textbook

To Bob Moog, for his important articles and inventions

To Paul Garrity of ARTEC and Carnegie-Mellon University, for his system design and consultation

To David Gray, Tom Watson, Rick Raymond and John Taylor III, for the MIDI research

To Mike Klein, Geoffrey Wilson, Will Becker, Chuck Bowen, David Jones, Tim O'Connell, Jeff Hickman and Jacques Woodin for their help and advice

To Charlie Richmond, for his leadership as the first USITT Sound Commissioner, boosting audio to a level that balances the other technical elements of production

To the Cape Cod Melody Tent, for my first professional experience in stage sound

And finally to Professor Travis Bogard and Professor Henry May at UC Berkeley, who taught me what is meant by art in the theatre

Illustrations

Note on the text

This book was written over the past few years in response to the needs of students in a class on audio practice. Perhaps no text becomes obsolete as quickly as one on sound. In an effort to keep up with the latest technology, research folders were created for each unit of study. Reference books and contemporary articles were used to update and maintain these subject files.

The chapters are organized so that fundamental principles are presented first. Ideas are developed in a cumulative way. Chapter 1 considers the nature of sound waves, Chapter 2 describes common inputs and outputs. The complexity grows gradually— Chapter 8 presents the inner workings of a compact disc player and Chapter 13 considers how those sound waves described in the first chapter may be sampled and stored digitally. Conventional pieces of equipment and procedures are covered, including microphones, turntables, loudspeakers, recording, splicing, and how to design a sound plot. In addition, there are sections on sequencers, signal processing gear, fiber optics, DAT and digital effects processors. The core, however, consists of the basic elements of stage sound and the things that one needs to know to create and maintain the audio environment in the theatre.

If this book is used in an undergraduate course, the first eleven chapters should be the minimum syllabus. Chapters 12 and 13 might be offered to the more advanced student, or selected elements may be covered as time permits. Those two chapters may be more difficult, since it is assumed that a technical vocabulary has been acquired by that time. Of course, while considering MIDI and computers, the instruction may be accelerated with a student who has worked with that kind of equipment since high school. Chapter 14, "Acoustics," and Chapter 15, "Intercom" are optional given the constraints of a one-semester course. These chapters may be useful to those who are involved in the planning or designing of a facility. In any case, the readings should be accompanied by lectures, demonstrations and workshops. Theory may be taught in the classroom but there is no substitute for practical experience to acquire real skills. Some chapters offer a "Practicum" at the end where projects are suggested for further investigation.

Since this is a book about technology, readers may be interested in how it was assembled. The text was written in Microsoft Word and typesetting was done with Ventura Desktop Publisher on an IBM PS/2 Model 80. Figures #1, 14, 15, 20, 23, 24, 29, 30, 35, 37, 38, 42, 44 and 45 were drawn by the author using Microsoft Paintbrush, converted from PCX to IMG files and imported into Ventura frames. Figures #8, 9 and 31 were scanned using a Houston Instruments DMP-60 plotter with SCAN-CAD accessory. The scanned plates were edited in AutoCad, then stored as DXF files. The DXF files were converted into GEM files using a utility. Then, the GEM files were brought into the text and modified using Ventura's graphics function. Some might argue that this is a convoluted method, going from raster to vector and back to raster. Other techniques were tried, but, given the constraints of time and equipment, the ones listed above proved to be the most successful.

The rest of the figures are photographs or were captured the old-fashioned way, using traditional photocopy techniques. Permission to reproduce these plates was granted from many excellent sources listed in the Acknowledgment and Bibliography.

Table of Contents

Introduction

The audio aspect of theatre production has never been as complex as it is today. Directors, designers and technicians are confronted with numerous choices concerning reinforcement, recording, playback and special effects. Acoustic experts measure, test, tune and modify spaces to be acceptable to the trained listener's ear. The audio specialist is earning a place in the theatre as the latest member of the collaborative artistic team.

On the stage, not only the physics, but the psychological properties of sound become important. The effect sound has in the theatre cannot be explained by mechanics alone. In addition to the physical cause, there is the physiological sensation which elicits a psychological response in the audience. The object is to move the audience, to create a world, suggest an environment, evoke an emotion, reveal truth. The ability of sound to reinforce a dramatic theme has been recognized by playwrights and directors for a long time. Communicating that idea to an audience accustomed to great fidelity at home and in the concert hall is a challenge for the sound designer, engineer and acoustician.

In every respect, the classical age represents the apotheosis of architectural and dramatic ideas. Every seat in the Greek and Roman theatre had a good view. The acoustics were perfect, so superb that the slightest sound on stage was heard by everyone. Epidaurus, the best preserved of the ancient theatres, built around 350 B.C., has extraordinary acoustic properties. This can be verified even today. A common match struck in the orchestra in front of the thymele will be heard perfectly from the highest vantage point among the 14,000 seats.

Another theatre of antiquity that has excellent acoustics is the Hellenistic theatre at Pergamum in Turkey. Built on a mountainside like a trembling reminder of another age, it is the steepest theatre in the world with seats at a 45-degree pitch. The Romans modified it in 160 B.C., adding sound towers at the top. Roman architects were noted for the effectiveness of their acoustics. Theatres and public buildings were all positioned for maximum sound efficiency. This theatre has a special advantage for high fidelity sound. Prevailing breezes that blow in from the sea each afternoon in theatre season not only provide an effective form of air-conditioning, but these winds carried with them the actors' voices up to the audience seated on the hillside.

The *First Folio* of Shakespeare includes stage directions such as "alarums, excursions, flourish, trumpets and drums," especially in the history plays when the French and English armies engage in battle. The Prologue of *Henry V* contains a reference to the actual stage and the illusion that must be conveyed:

> may we cram
> Within this wooden O the very casques
> That did affright the air of Agincourt.
>
> Think, when we talk of horses, that you see them
> Printing their proud hoofs i' the receiving earth.

Gordon Craig, the great designer and prophet of the New Stagecraft, claimed that drama died when it went indoors. He expressed many complaints with prevailing theatre practice in his day and some of the problems may have been acoustic ones traceable to the evolution of the indoor performing space. In the sixteenth century, scholars looked to the Roman architect Vitruvius for models. Palladio designed the Teatro Olimpico in a semi-oval auditorium where staged academic readings took place in front of a richly decorated *scaenae frons* backed with doorways revealing the *papier maché* perspectives finished by Scamozzi. Aleotti created the first permanent proscenium arch in the U-shaped Teatro Farnese at Parma. The horseshoe-shaped auditorium with tiered seats and an orchestra "pit" was the norm from the baroque age until the nineteenth century. Since the middle of the seventeenth century when Italian opera burst upon Europe, theatres have been designed almost exclusively in a way best suited to operatic performances. Even Moliere performed in front of wing and border sets at the Palais-Royal.

Exactly what is meant by the modern theatre as perceived by Craig is:

> The whole result as heard and seen on the stage: play, music, scene, acting, dancing, lighting, singing—all.

Craig and Adolphe Appia are often mentioned together as torch-bearers of a new aesthetic. In his book *Music and the Stage Setting*, first published in 1899, Appia stresses the relationship between music and the plastic qualities of directional lighting. He reaches the conclusion that the arrangement of the stage is to be found in the rhythm of the music. Appia shows in detail, through analysis of the music-drama of Richard Wagner, that spatial forms are dictated by the nature and quality of the sound.

The importance of sound effects on stage and behind the scenes was realized by the Duke of Saxe-Meiningen, who revolutionized theatre production methods in the nineteenth century. The Meininger were noted for many innovations including the shrewd use of sound effects to heighten the emotional impact of the drama. Sound was used to reinforce the mood and elevate the activity of the imagination. His Berlin production of Schiller's *Fiesko* had a number of sounds: alarm bells heralding an assault, weapons pounding against iron-studded crossbars, axe-blows splintering heavy gates, explosions, bomb blasts, the clash of swords fading in the distance.

Stanislavski used a sound recording to solve a dramatic problem. In *My Life in Art*, he describes the staggering lesson he was given by a woman whom the Moscow Art Theatre brought back to Moscow in 1902 as a consultant on the milieu of *The Power of Darkness*:

> She interpreted the inner and outer contents of Tolstoy's tragedy so fully, truthfully, and in such bright colors, she justified each of our Naturalistic details of production to such an

extent that she became irreplaceable to us. But when she left the stage and the regular actors of the company were on, their spiritual and physical imitation betrayed them...We made a final trial. We did not let her come on, but made her sing in the wings. But even this was dangerous for the actors. Then we made a phonograph record of her voice, and her song provided a background for the action without breaking up our ensemble.

Guillaume Apollinaire's surrealist drama *Les Mamelles de Tirésias* takes place in front of the people of Zanzibar represented by a single actor who never speaks. Instead, he sits at a table stocked with devices for the production of noises—guns, drums, castanets, pots and pans. The preface to the play describes the dramatist's world:

> His universe is the play
> Within which he is God the Creator
> Who disposes at will
> Of sounds gestures movements masses colors
> Not merely in order
> To photograph what is called a slice of life
> But to bring forth life itself in all its truth

Eugene O'Neill's *Emperor Jones* has a tom-tom accompaniment to the play. In the original production by the Provincetown Players this rhythmic device, which began at the beat of the normal heart, rose in tempo and volume until it filled the tiny Provincetown Playhouse with an ocean of sustained intensity and lifted the hearers out of their seats. Sound can have a powerful affective value in the theatre. It may even help to distract attention from flaws in a script.

Mordecai Gorelik, in his comprehensive treatise *New Theatres for Old*, provides several examples of dramatic sound effects in the plays of Eugene O'Neill. In his 1922 play *The Hairy Ape*, the most powerful scene is that of the stokehole, with its noise, glaring furnaces, frightful heat and piercing whistles. The syncopated crunching of coal serves as an essential choral accompaniment.

Lee Simonson, in his book *The Stage is Set*, exhibits a memorandum sent by O'Neill to the Theatre Guild in 1929,

4

shortly before his play *Dynamo* went into rehearsal. O'Neill comments on the importance of sound to his play. In this case the effects are thunder and lightning in Part One, and the sound of the water flowing over the near-by dam and the hum of the generator in Part Two:

> I cannot stress too emphatically the importance of starting early in rehearsals to get these [sound] effects exactly right. It must be realized that these are not incidental noises but significant dramatic overtones that are an integral part of that composition in the theatre which is the whole play. If they are dismissed until the last dress rehearsals (the usual procedure in my experience), then the result must inevitably be an old melodrama thunderstorm, and a generator sounding obviously like a vacuum cleaner; not only will the true values of these effects be lost but they will make the play look foolish.

> I may seem to be a bug on the subject of sound in the theatre—but I have a reason. Someone once said that the difference between my plays and other contemporary work was that I always wrote primarily by ear for the ear, that most of my plays, even down to the rhythm of the dialogue, had the definite structural quality of a musical composition. The point here is that I have always used sound in plays as a structural part of them. This is a machine age which one would like to express as a background for lines in plays in overtones of characteristic, impelling and governing mechanical sound and rhythm—but how can one, unless a corresponding mechanical perfection in the theatre is a reliable string of the instrument (the theatre as a whole) on which one composes?

> Looking back on my plays in which significant mechanical sound and not music is called for (nearly all of the best ones) I can say that none of them has ever really been thoroughly done in the modern theatre although they were written for it. Some day I hope they will be—and people are due to be surprised by the added dramatic value—modern values—they will take on.

Today, when some sort of sound is used in nearly every production from the lavish Broadway musical to regional outdoor revivals, attention to this technical element is increasingly important. Accurate and appropriate sound reproduction is a requirement for every successful production. The new theatre artist must be able to create a dramatic idea with sound. Audience members are accustomed to exceptional audio clarity in the concert hall, the cinema and at home. Directors and designers agree that the audience should expect the same or better in the theatre. The sound designer must be capable of reinforcing the quietest whisper as well as the loudest crash in order to sustain the dramatic moment. While we look to the past for models, we must look to the present and future for the technology to realize those goals.

1. Sound Waves and Frequencies

Definition

Sound is the movement of air in the form of pressure waves that travel 1130 feet per second. Solids, liquids and gases will transmit sound waves, but a vacuum will not. Sound requires a medium of transmission.

Frequency

The back and forth motion of a piston creates a pressure wave. Refer to Figure 1 to see the analogous behavior of a rock on a string being dipped into a pool of water. The displacement and the rate of this reciprocating piston governs the curve of the pressure wave. Sound is created by a reciprocating motion of a piston in air. Frequency is defined as the number of times the pressure wave passes through a complete cycle in one second. In the case of the rock, the frequency of dips determines the wavelength. The size of the

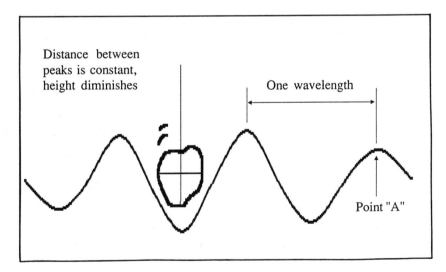

Figure 1. Sound waves represented by stone in pool

rock determines the initial amplitude of the waves. Point "A" shows that as the waves travel away from the source, they diminish in height (intensity), but the wavelength remains constant. One cycle consists of the distance between peaks, a complete cycle being from peak to trough to peak. The number of cycles per second (CPS) determines the frequency of the sound. The amplitude of the waves determines loudness. In 1965, the term cycles per second was changed to Hertz (Hz) in honor of Heinrich Rudolf Hertz, an early German physicist. One cycle per second is stated as 1 Hz; 1 kilocycle as 1 kHz; 1 megacycle as 1 MHz. Either CPS or Hz may be used, but Hz is preferred. Human hearing extends from 20 to 20,000 Hz (20 kHz). A young, healthy ear is sensitive to the full range, but as a person gets older, sensitivity to the high end decreases. A normal adult may have an upper frequency limit of 14,000 Hz.

If a frequency is doubled or halved, that represents one octave. Frequencies between 16 and 32 Hz are called the first octave and are heard in the lowest tones of an organ. This range is also called the threshold of feeling. Frequencies between 32 and 512 Hz are considered the second through fifth octaves. The rhythmic low and upper bass frequencies are in this area.

The sixth and seventh octaves are from 512 to 2048 Hz. If speech is limited to this frequency range, the sound will have a tinny, telephone quality. Over accentuation of these frequencies will cause listener fatigue. Emphasizing the eighth and ninth octaves, 2048 to 8192 Hz, adds presence to the sound. The human ear approaches its maximum sensitivity between 2000 and 4000 Hz. Lip and breath sounds are within this range and can be controlled through equalization.

The tenth octave consists of the region between 8192 and 16,000 Hz. These are responsible for brilliance in the sound. The tinkling of bells, triangle, cymbals and wind chimes are sounds that will benefit from emphasis of this octave.

White noise is not an individual frequency, but contains all sounds perceptible to the human ear. It is analogous to white light which contains all of the wavelengths in the light spectrum. The white noise waveform is sawtooth-shaped and consists of a fundamental frequency and even harmonics. It is not useful for calibration since the individual frequencies are not reproduced at equal energy levels.

1. Sound Waves and Frequencies

Pink noise is similar to white noise, but, instead of a rising intensity, all frequencies are reproduced at an equal energy level. This makes measurement convenient. Pink noise is used by a Real Time Analyzer (RTA) for on-site audio spectrum analysis of sound reinforcement systems. The pink noise reproduced by the loudspeakers is detected by a microphone connected to the RTA. Individual frequency bands are displayed in real time, and the data may be used to determine an optimal equalization curve for the environment.

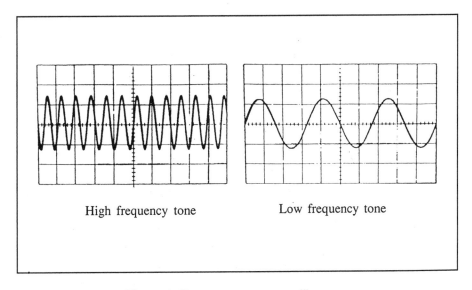

High frequency tone   Low frequency tone

Figure 2. Pure tones on an oscilloscope

Pure tones can be generated by an oscillator built into a mixing board or tape player. A tone can be displayed on an oscilloscope as shown in Figure 2. Notice the sine wave characteristic. The wave rises from zero to maximum in one direction, returns to zero in a symmetrical pattern, reverses direction and falls below zero to an equal magnitude, and returns to zero during one complete cycle.

Sound for the Stage

Sound is not always composed of a single frequency wave. It usually consists of many frequencies existing simulatneously. The table below gives a range of frequencies for musical instruments and other common sounds.

Cymbals	340—12,000 Hz
Snare Drum	70—15,000 Hz
Tympani	40—5500 Hz
Violin	180—8000 Hz
Piano	60—8000 Hz
Flute	250—9000 Hz
Trumpet	160—10,000 Hz
Trombone	70—7500 Hz
Female Speech	170—10,000 Hz
Male Speech	100—8500 Hz
Hand Clapping	100—16,000 Hz
Footsteps	70—15,000 Hz

Pitch

Pitch is the property of a musical tone determined by its frequency and intensity. The higher the frequency, the higher the pitch. Tuning to a pitch is also a matter of subjective taste. Today there is a controversy over the proper frequency to tune a violin. When Stradivari and other Cremonese masters were making their violins almost 300 years ago, everyone agreed that the pitch of A above middle C was around 420 CPS or 420 Hz. Since A is the tuning note on which other notes are based, first A is tuned in, then all strings are tightened accordingly. With A at 420, violins sounded warm and rich among the few other strings in a small chamber orchestra. As orchestras and concert halls got larger, musicians started to tune sharper, raising the pitch of A and therefore all other notes. During the life of Verdi, A was sharpened to 435 Hz at an international meeting in Vienna. In 1939, A was established at 440, corresponding to the 49th key on a standard 88-note piano. Currently, the demand is for even higher tunings of 443, 445, 450 and even 460 Hz.

1. Sound Waves and Frequencies

Timbre

Timbre is used to describe the characteristic quality of a musical instrument which allows it to be differentiated from another. Timbre depends upon overtones or harmonics. If all of the harmonics are removed by the use of filters, all instruments will sound the same, except for the pitch.

dB

A decibel, or dB is a logarithmic ratio of intensities. The sound levels encountered in daily life are numerous and vary over a large range of sound pressures. The dB measures SPL, or sound pressure level, which is normally calculated by expressing the sound pressure level with respect to a reference sound pressure, generally 0.0002 microbar for airborne sound. A more helpful relative indication of dB is charted below:

dB	Environmental Equivalent
140	Jet aircraft at takeoff
130	"Heavy metal" concert
120	Noisy subway station
110	Machine shop
100	Large symphony orchestra
90	Cannery
80	Inside a moving car
70	Office meeting
60	Conversational speech
50	Average residence
40	Quiet neighborhood
30	Study in private home
20	Empty theatre
10	Inside a recording studio
0	Inside an anechoic chamber

Fletcher-Munson Observations

In the 1930s two researchers at the Bell Telephone Laboratories named Fletcher and Munson plotted a group of sensitivity curves for the human ear showing its characteristic for different intensity levels between the threshold of hearing and the threshold of feeling. The curves have been refined more recently by Robinson and Dadson. These data are often referred to as equal loudness contours. The reference frequency is 1000 Hz. Referring to Figure 3, it is clear that the contours are not equally spaced, but converge at the lower frequencies. This characteristic causes a change in the quality of reproduced sound when the volume level is changed. If it is desired to have two pure tones of equal loudness, for instance 1000 Hz and 50 Hz, and the 1000 Hz tone has an intensity level of plus 80 dB, following the curve out to 50 Hz indicates that an intensity level of plus 85 dB is required to make the 50

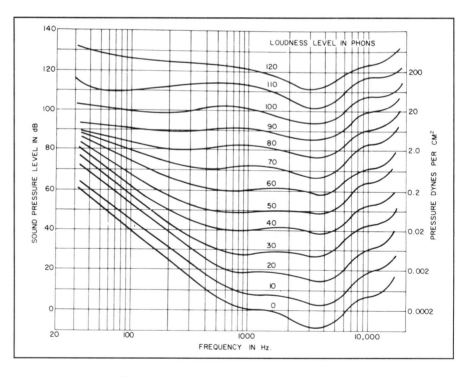

Figure 3. Fletcher-Munson observations

1. Sound Waves and Frequencies

Hz tone sound as loud as the 1000 Hz tone, or a difference of 5 dB. If you lower the gain to where the 1000 Hz tone has an intensity level of plus 40 dB, following the curve out to 50 Hz, it can be seen that the intensity of this frequency must be increased to 72 dB to equal the loudness of the 1000 Hz tone, or an increase of 32 dB. Note that in lowering the level, the balance between the low and mid range frequencies has been destroyed, and to the ear it appears that the low frequency response is lacking. This is the principal reason for including a loudness control in home reproducing equipment. This also means that a monitor level in the studio must be established and maintained for consistency in recording.

Doppler Effect

An approaching ambulance siren appears to be higher pitched and louder than a receding siren. After passing the observer, the pitch and intensity drop quite rapidly until the sound fades completely. As the source approaches the listener, more cycles per second are being received than when it is going away. The increase in pitch is caused by compression of the sound wave as a result of the forward motion of the ambulance being added to the velocity of the sound wave. Conversely, as the ambulance moves away from the observer, the pitch decreases because the speed of recession is subtracted from the normal velocity of the sound wave, resulting in a lower pitch.

Reverberation

Reverberation occurs when sound is reflected several times between the surfaces of an enclosed space before reaching the ear. If it is greater than about 1.5 seconds, then direct speech tends to overlap and intelligibility is impaired. Both speech and music will be blurred and may become unintelligible because successive sounds overlap.

Phasing

The two components of phase are time and frequency. Different wavelengths will cancel each other out depending on the time of arrival and the frequency. It is possible to adjust the acoustic environment to reinforce a frequency. Similarly, it is also possible for frequencies to cancel each other out.

Standing waves occur when a sustained tone is emitted in an enclosure consisting of parallel walls. Anyone moving through the space will experience the sensation of an increase and decrease in the intensity of the sound, since the listener is passing through the zero and maximum points of the waves. Standing waves may be prevented by nonparallel walls, convex surfaces, multilevel ceiling sections and diffusers on the walls and ceilings.

A binaural head, which is a mannequin's head with microphones placed at the ear positions, may be used to determine the effects of phasing on the listener. The binaural head will only work for frequencies above 700 Hz, since lower wavelengths are so long that they seem to arrive simultaneously in phase.

In addition to the acoustic component, phase cancellation may also occur due to electrical problems in the hookup of loudspeakers or in the alignment of the drivers. See Chapter 5 for more on that type of phasing.

1. Sound Waves and Frequencies

Practicum

1. Play a test tape on a tape player and listen to pure tones at reference level.

2. Take a signal from the oscillator of a mixing board or tape recorder and route it through speakers with a constant gain. Then vary the frequency and observe what happens to sound perception. Notice how you must increase the intensity to hear low frequencies at the same level (Fletcher-Munson).

2. Inputs and Outputs

Basic Electricity

There are two subatomic particles associated with electricity, but electricity is not atomic energy. The negatively charged electron moves about in the flow of electricity. The positively charged proton remains more or less fixed, providing the attraction that makes the electrons flow. Electricity is generated by detaching electrons from the atoms of materials by the application of energy, leaving the atoms in a state of unbalance; that is, there are more protons than electrons, and the result is a positive charge. Meanwhile, the extra energy which has detached the electrons causes them to accumulate at what is called the "negative" terminal. The difficulty comes in understanding that the electrons flow from a place of negative charge to a place of positive charge. In this sense the term "negative" denotes a surplus of electrons and the term "positive," a shortage.

Not all materials part easily with electrons from their atoms to produce a flow of electrons. Those materials that do allow electron flow are called conductors. Their electrons are detached easily and little energy is lost. Other materials part with electrons only with difficulty and with considerable loss of energy in the form of heat. These materials are known as poor conductors. Still other materials will release only a few electrons under any conditions. Such materials, called insulators, are used to isolate conductors from each other to keep electricity where we want it.

The basic pattern of any electrical circuit is: surplus of electrons, flow path, return to electron source. The elements of a circuit include:

1. a generator of electricity
2. a conductor to allow the electrons to flow
3. insulation to keep the electrons in the path
4. something to use the electrical energy
5. return conductor to allow electrons
   back to the generator

17

Impedance

Impedance is similar to resistance but the term impedance is reserved for use with alternating current (AC). For limiting the amount of current passing a given point, we can use resistors, inductors and capacitors. The unit of resistance used when measuring the resistance of resistors and the impedance of inductors and capacitors is called an ohm. Inductors and capacitors have another very important property in electronic circuits in that they have different effects on low and high frequencies. A simple tone control could consist of a selection of capacitors connected across the signal wires. Depending upon which capacitor is chosen, more or less of the high frequencies would be shorted out relative to the low frequencies.

Balanced and Unbalanced Lines

In addition to the voltage and impedance at inputs and outputs of equipment, we also need to know whether the connections are balanced or unbalanced. An unbalanced system uses interconnecting cables with one conductor and an overall braided screen, whereas a balanced system has two conductors plus a screen. It follows that plugs and receptacles for unbalanced systems need two pins or connections while for a balanced system three are required.

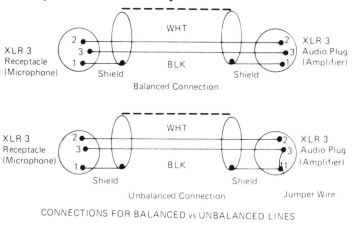

CONNECTIONS FOR BALANCED vs UNBALANCED LINES

Figure 5

Figure 4. Balanced vs. Unbalanced connections

2. Inputs and Outputs

XLR, 1/4"Phone Plug, RCA and Other Connectors

The weakest link in any audio system is the interconnection between components. Expensive mixers, amplifiers and loudspeakers must be linked with cable and connectors. Faulty connections are responsible for a majority of sound problems. In order to ensure a solid connection, it is best to use a locking connector, such as a 3-pin XLR connector made by Switchcraft. These are used primarily for balanced lines and are often referred to as microphone or Cannon connectors.

Phone jack plugs are available in 2- and 3-pole configurations. It is a standard 1/4" plug and often used for connections between mixer and amp, or between mixer and effects or signal processing equipment. Patch panels may have jack fields designed for the 1/4" phone plug. Some loudspeakers have a 1/4" jack, but it is recommended that a locking connector be used for theatrical loudspeakers. A two-pin twist lock connector is ideal for this purpose.

A loudspeaker or amplifier may have binding posts or banana jack receptacles. A problem with banana jacks is that they lose their spring after a while and must be "tweaked" to fit snugly. Again, it is recommended that the loudspeaker be converted to a locking connector.

The RCA-type jack, also called a phono plug connector, is commonly found for line input and output on home audio equipment. It may be seen on the back plate of many cassette decks, CD players or integrated amplifiers. Molded plastic versions are available, but it is preferable to use the soldered metal plugs and jacks if you must use this type of connector.

Adapters are to be avoided as much as possible. Occasionally a converter may be needed with rented or borrowed equipment. But they are to be used with caution. An adapter may be matching two pieces of equipment without matching the impedance. Do not use an adapter to go from 3-pin XLR to 2-pin phone jack without using a line-matching transformer to go from low to high impedance or vice versa.

Wire and Cable

Microphone cables are vulnerable and must be handled with care. "Elbow wrapping" should be avoided since it forces tremendous twists and strains which may result in internal breakage. When wrapping cable, try to determine the natural way it wants to coil. Once in awhile, mic cable can be brought up to the grid in order to let it unwind and find its own shape. Then it is much easier to coil. Cable may be stored on pegs and color coded by length. When traveling with mic cables, use a case and store the cables without mic stands or any other equipment that may damage the cable. Remember, the most sophisticated equipment in the world will not work unless the cable and connectors have integrity (and continuity).

Multiconnectors and Snakes

Multicord cable is invaluable for sound reinforcement applications where a lot of microphones are used. Snakes can be made to your custom configuration by companies such as Wireworks. You may specify how many XLR or 1/4" phone plugs are on each end. You may have individual connectors on the mixer end of the snake and a box with receptacles on the stage end. Customized snakes are a key component in live stage applications.

Fiber Optics

Optical fibers consist of a core material which carries the light, surrounded by a layer of cladding that reflects the light within the core. This reflection allows the signal to be transmitted through the optical fiber. Long-distance transmission systems use fibers with glass cores, referred to as "all-glass fibers." Fibers which use a glass core to carry light, but have a plastic or polymer cladding are called PCS (Polymer Clad Silica) fibers.

Fiber optics offer several advantages over metallic systems. The transmitted signals are not distorted by any form of outside electronic, magnetic or radio frequency interference. Optical systems are immune to lightning or high voltage interference. They do not require grounding connections; the transmitter and receiver are electrically isolated and free from ground loop problems.

The simplest link consists of an optical transmitter and receiver connected by a length of optical cable. The optical transmitter converts the electronic signal voltage into optical power which is launched into the fiber by a light emitting diode (LED), laser diode (LD) or laser. The optical pulses are converted by a photodetector directly into a desired electrical signal. This process is closely analogous to the way old-fashioned crystal radios detected broadcast signals. A new approach, coherent communications, involves the use of two lasers, one at each end of the fiber optic link, plus the photodetector diode.

Ground rules are being established to guide the technology in an orderly manner. One area in which a standard is rapidly nearing completion and industry is already producing components, is the Fiber Distributed Data Interface (FDDI). This will likely become something like the computer standard interface RS-232, or the MIDI of fiber optics.

Earth Loops and Shielding

When unbalanced equipment is connected, the screen of the cable which is carrying the signal links the cases of the mixer and amplifier. Both cases may be connected to earth for safety creating a continuous, circular path from the earth at one mains plug, through the mains cable to the mixer, through the mixer chassis to the screen of the link cable to the amplifier chassis, and back to earth via the amplifier mains cable. Then, this earth current combines with the signal in the cable giving hum in the background of the signal. The earth loop can be broken (see Figure 5) by disconnecting the earth wire in all but one of the mains plugs. This can be dangerous but may be justifiable in a permanent installation where the equipment is earthed by the screened cables.

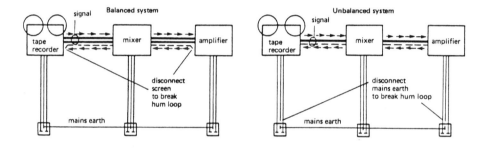

Figure 5. Disconnecting earth loop

Buzzes, Pops and Clicks

Microphone cables are particularly susceptible to all forms of electrical interference. It is important that these cables be kept clear of all power cables, such as those used for lighting instruments. It may appear convenient to wrap loudspeaker or mic cable along with lighting cable to "trim" the offstage areas, but this can be deadly to a sound system. It might cause the sound system to modulate those electrostatic and electromagnetic induced currents. If your speakers "vroom" when the lights are dimmed, you had better start looking for AC cables that are in close proximity to your sound cables.

Another problem comes when "hot-patching" amplifiers and speakers. This should be avoided at all costs. If you must re-patch, turn the amp off first. Otherwise, you run the risk of causing your ears a great deal of harm, and blowing up the amp in the meantime. Never unplug a speaker while it is being driven by an amp as the amplifier may self-destruct.

Troubleshooting

The simplest way to trace any problem is to start at the amplifier and work back to the mixer. It also helps to have a headset to check the signal from the source, then the mixer, and so on until you can determine where the signal is being hurt. Above all, don't panic. Try to develop a systematic approach to troubleshooting. It may be something obvious, like a component coming unplugged or a patching problem. If you start simply and analyze your signal path carefully, you will at least be able to identify the problem.

Hum: The sound of 60-cycle current and its harmonics (120 Hz, 240 Hz, etc.) produces hum, which can be introduced into the signal path. Check all of the connections, jiggling the cable ends to detect changes in tone. If the hum stops or changes frequency, you have isolated the problem. If it is a molded plug, cut it off and replace it with a new connector. A nonmolded plug can be resoldered. RCA plugs can be fixed by pressing the outer ground "petals" inward. Cables can also introduce hum. Check to make sure that all cables are grounded and routed away from all AC lines. Keep power cables as short as possible. Avoid coiling power cable near components as it may create an "electron field." Do not stack pre-amps on or near power amps as the transformers in the power amplifiers may induce hum into a pre-amp's circuits. If all else fails, equalization may be able to eliminate some frequencies, but remember that the signal will contain some desirable frequencies that may be cut or rolled off by EQ. If the hum is inherent in the component itself, like a noisy mixer or piece of signal processing gear, have a qualified technician analyze the circuits. An intermittent filter capacitor or failing transistor may be part of the problem.

Feedback: The sudden shriek that occurs when a singer points the microphone into the loudspeaker is an annoying and embarrassing experience for the sound engineer. Proper placement of main and monitor speakers may reduce the potential for feedback. Always do a sound check to determine how much "headroom" you have on each potentiometer. Mark these levels carefully. Know when you will approach feedback levels. Finally, power up gradually and check the microphones one at a time to have control. You will then be able to react quickly with the correct response if you hear a sudden squeal.

Pops: Turning the mixer on after the amps have been powered up will produce a nasty "pop" in the audio system. Another cause is the vocalist that gets too close to the microphone. The combination of plosive "p" and the proximity effect of increased bass may cause a potentially disastrous problem for the loudspeakers. Use windscreens or acoustic filters on the microphones. Turn on the mixer before the power amps and turn off the power amps before the mixer.

Crackles and buzzes: Pushing loudspeakers into distortion with too much signal or dirty potentiometers creates a static that irritates the senses and may destroy the speaker. Use a cleaner for potentiometer contacts. Avoid transients that may overdrive the speakers. Look for bad contacts between connectors.

RF interference: Radio frequencies may be induced from lighting dimmers, nearby transmitter towers or AC noise. Use heavy duty shielded cable. Check all ground connections and isolate dimmer and lighting cables from audio lines. Avoid ground loops.

A cable tester is an invaluable piece of test equipment to keep on hand. It is relatively easy to build one, but there are

2. Inputs and Outputs

products available that are ideal for that purpose. The Whirlwind Tester (Figure 6) is a comprehensive cable testing device that is compact and comes with a belt clip for convenience. On the tester there are 5 LEDs, 2 XLR jacks, 2 1/4" jacks, 2 RCA (phono) jacks and one power switch. To test cables, it is only necessary to connect both ends of the cable according to the routing diagrams. The LEDs will light to indicate polarity and continuity. When one or more of the LEDs fail to light, the cable may be considered bad.

Figure 6. Cable tester (Courtesy Whirlwind Music Dist.,Inc.)

When testing XLR cables, all three green LEDs will light when the cable is good. If pins 2 and 3 are reversed on an XLR connector, the red LED labeled PHASE REVERSE will light. If there is an open ground (pin 1), no LEDs will light. Readings for 1/4" cables are much the same. When using mono cables, the LED labeled PIN 2/RING will not light, since it corresponds to the ring on a stereo plug. RCA cables are tested using the 2 LEDs marked PHONO, with the top

LED corresponding to ground and the bottom corresponding to hot. The device also has provisions for testing special adapter cables.

Proper connection, grounding, high signal-to-noise ratios and periodic maintenance to clean pots and demagnetize heads may solve most of your noise problems. A lot of old graphic equalizers may add more noise, instead of improving the sound. Switch the EQ out of the system if you are not using it. When dubbing, patch the tape recorders directly together instead of running them through a mixer. Use dbx or other noise reduction whenever possible. A noise gate may also help eliminate what little noise is left. And then you can sit back and enjoy your sound emerging from total silence.

3. Mixing Consoles

A mixer is a device that accepts signals from several inputs and then feeds a common sound distribution system. The signal sources may consist of taped dialogue, music, sound effects or a live microphone pickup. Several separate audio signal sources are combined into one composite signal or group of signals. An operator controls the signal from an input by means of switches, levers and knobs, and then routes the signal to recorders, special effects devices or power amplifiers. Mixers are specified by the number of inputs and outputs. As an example, an 8 x 2 mixer will have eight inputs and two outputs, a 16 x 2 x 8 mixer will have sixteen inputs, two main outputs and eight submaster outputs. The versatility and complexity of the system increases with the number of input and output channels.

Each channel usually has its own preamplifier and tone controls. Mixers may be active or passive. Passive mixers use resistors and potentiometers, active mixers use amplifiers along with resistors to control gain or attenuation. The operator controls the relative levels of microphones, adjusts tone and selects the output destination. Auxiliary inputs and outputs may be used for special effects and monitor mixes. The stereo image of the sound is adjusted by balancing the amount of signal in each of the output channels. Movement of the sound may be accomplished in a similar way.

Most mixers amplify the signal from each microphone and add the amplified signal together to produce a single output that feeds a power amplifier and then loudspeakers. Each doubling of the number of microphones reduces the available gain before feedback by 3 dB. A large system may present a problem if the operator is not adept at operating faders and switching channels in and out of the system. Sometimes the feedback will expand so rapidly that the operator doesn't have time to respond. If the operator is not able to determine which microphone is causing the problem, the entire system must be shut down.

Sound for the Stage

In the 1970s the concept of automatic microphone mixers was developed. A simple gate was inserted into each channel to shut the microphone down when it was not being used. These were called "NOM=1" automatic mixers because the gain of the system was always adjusted to equal the gain with one open microphone. Newer automatic mixers, such as the Altec Lansing model 1678C, use expansion instead of gating. This permits more versatile operation to hold mixer gain to the equivalent of one single microphone under constantly changing conditions.

Figure 7 shows a Soundcraft Series 800 B mixing console. This is not an automatic mixer, but a traditional resistive network consisting of 16 inputs, 2 main outputs and 8 submaster outputs. The input modules are specifically designed for theatre. A detailed description of the input and output channels of this mixer follows.

Figure 7. Soundcraft Series 800B mixing console

3. Mixing Consoles

The Input Channel

The input channel can be operated in either microphone or line input modes. The microphone input impedance is greater than 2 k ohms, which will not cause any loading effects on normal microphones. The high level line input is unbalanced, with an input impedance of greater than 10 k ohms.

Pressing the PAD button (1a) inserts a 20 dB attenuator into the input of the microphone amplifier.

The MIC TRIM control (1b) is a detented potentiometer which can be varied between 20 dB and 55 dB of gain.

The LINE TRIM gain (1c) can be varied between -10 dB and +20 dB using a detented potentiometer.

The high level Line Input is selected by pressing the LI button (1d).

Pressing the phase button (1e) will invert the phase on the input to correct for any mismatch.

Capacitor microphones can be powered by the internal +48-volt power supply by pressing the PWR button (1f). When using Direct Injection boxes, or unbalanced sources, the phantom power supply should not be switched on.

The input meter (1g), comprised of discrete LEDs, will indicate the input level as selected by the Mic/Line switch.

Pressing the MTR button (1h) will place the input meter into the signal path.

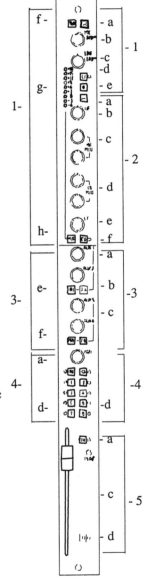

Figure 8. Input Module

29

The equalizer section (2 a-f) allows five areas of control over the audio spectrum.

The auxiliary section (3 a-d) contains four auxiliary send controls. Each control can be routed to two auxiliary mix buses to give a total of eight auxiliary sends for use as echo, foldback or other effects.

The routing section (4 a-d) lets the channel input signal be routed to any or all of the eight group outputs and the stereo mix, by selecting the relevant routing button.

The Pan Pot (4a) is a center-detented control with a loss of 4.5 dB at that point. This is a compromise between the 3 dB loss required for constant power panning and the 6 dB loss required for constant voltage panning.

The Pan control may be placed in the signal path by pressing the PAN button (4b). When the Pan control is not in the signal path any signal routed via the MIX button appears at equal level both left and right.

By selecting the MIX button (4c), the signal is routed directly to the stereo mix bus.

The signal may be routed to any of Groups 1–8 by selecting the appropriate routing button (4d). When PAN is selected the Group routing is also fed via the Pan Pot. Panning left will feed Groups 1, 3, 5 and 7; panning right will feed Groups 2, 4, 6 and 8.

The channel ON status (5a) is indicated by a green LED.

A red LED (5b) indicates the peak signal level at the insert send point, and illuminates at a level of aproximately 4 dB below clipping.

The channel fader (5c) is a long throw linear device. Infinity cut-off is greater than 90 dB.

PFL (5d) solos the pre-fader, post insert jack signal independently of the ON switch. PFL operation is indicated by a red LED on the channel and master warning LED on the Master Module.

The Output Channel

The Soundcraft 8016 PA Output channel (Matrix) was designed primarily for theatre and stage monitor applications. The 8-way matrix output allows the operator to configure the subgroup fader to act as a master fader for up to eight other outputs. If you have multiple speakers at different levels, these can be preset using the matrix feature and controlled by moving just one potentiometer. Both the subgroup and matrix outputs are electronically balanced.

A signal derived either pre- or post- subgroup fader can be independently sent to any or all of the eight matrix outputs (1a).

For pre-fader sends the PRE button (1b) should be pressed.

A master level control (1c) is provided to adjust the overall level of the sum of all matrix sends to the matrix output. The output is switched into operation by selecting the ON button (1d). The matrix master signal can be soloed by depressing the AFL button (1e).

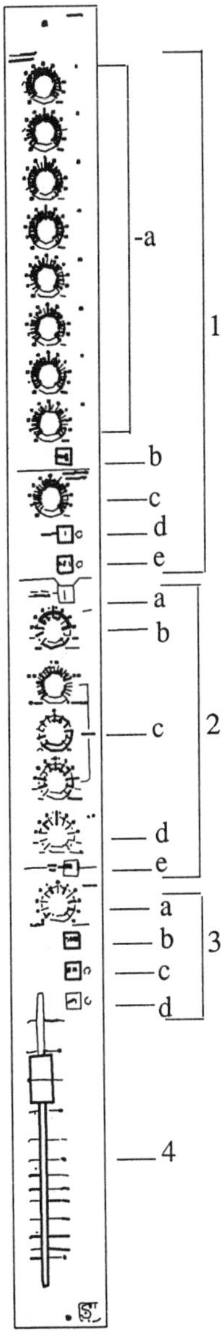

The 3-band equalizer section with shelving type bass and treble and a fully parametric midfrequency section may be inserted into the effects return signal path, or used normally in the subgroup position (2a-e). The shelving characteristic refers to the slope of the EQ curve. It does not keep rising

Figure 9. Output module

with frequency, but, having reached the desired amount, flattens out, or "shelves," from that frequency on.

The PAN control (3a) adjusts the relative balance of the subgroup signal into the stereo mix, if SUB (3b) has been selected. Selecting SUB routes the subgroup signal directly into the stereo mix, via the pan pot, without affecting the signal to the subgroup output.

Pressing the ON switch (3c) switches the subgroup into operation. A green LED indicates subgroup operation.

The group output signal can be soloed with the AFL switch (3d).

The channel fader (4) is a linear potentiometer.

The Direct Injection Box

In the age of electronic keyboards and other electrified musical instruments, a direct box is a mandatory piece of equipment. This device accepts an input signal that may be a high impedance or preamplified output. The direct box will then provide a balanced low impedance (150 ohms) signal for input to balanced low-Z equipment like a mixer or tape deck. The input is normally a 1/4" jack, as on the Whirlwind Director Direct Box. A loop-through 1/4" output is available as well as a male XLR jack for the balanced output. A switch which engages a -30 dB pad can be used for very hot instrument signals or for the speaker output of an amplifier. Another application is to route the output of a cinema projector through the DI box to the mixer and house sound system for improved fidelity. There is also a switch to insert a low-pass filter. The final feature, and one of the most important, is a ground lift switch which disconnects the ground between the input and balanced output.

3. Mixing Consoles

Digital Mixing

There are two types of digital mixing: digital-controlled and all-digital. The digital-controlled system is one where the program material is still processed in its analog form, but faders, mutes, routing and equalization are controlled by a microprocessor. The all-digital system has an A/D converter at each input on the console and the signals are processed digitally. Professional all-digital consoles like the Neve DSP may cost upwards of $750,000. Professional digitally-controlled mixers like the SSL Series 4000 or other MIDI-based systems are available. An "affordable" digital mixer is the Yamaha DMP7, which is an 8 x 2 (8 inputs, 2 outputs) listing for less than $4000. It is a console with real-time MIDI-based automation of all functions and contains three programmable digital effects processors. The mixer processes streams of 16-bit numbers with 24-bit internal computation and a 44.1 kHz sampling rate. Changes can be recorded and recalled in internal memory locations, or in real-time via MIDI on a sequencer. It can be used for mixdown and live applications, especially since all parameters can be operated by external MIDI Note On/Off and controller commands. It also has motorized faders. This digital mixer in its present form is a foreshadowing of things to come.

Practicum

1. Practice using the mixer in your theatre. Use microphone and line input sources, and experiment with equalization and routing functions.

2. Obtain a picture of the input or output module from the manual and label the various switches and knobs.

3. Try to insert effects with auxiliary paths. Learn the practical difference between pre- and post-send and return.

4. Power Amplifiers

An amplifier is an electrical circuit which transforms small voltages and currents into much larger ones with enough power to drive the cone of a loudspeaker.

At the heart of an amplifier is a device that controls flow-of-current on one terminal by a small voltage on an opposite terminal. This is analogous to a fast current of water controlled by a small force on the handle of a valve.

Vacuum tubes, transistors and magnetic fields are a few of the different devices used to accomplish this result. Some amplifiers are capable of amplifying a voltage (output) by as much as 100 times the original voltage (input). A good amplifier is capable of changing a soft sound or low intensity signal (such as one transformed by a dynamic mic) into a signal of much greater intensity than the original source.

Wattage and Rating

Amplifiers are rated using different factors for load and the results may mislead the user. If you see an amplifier advertised as providing 400 watts peak power, and another at 100 watts RMS, you may jump to the conclusion that the 400 watt amp has more power available. But you could be wrong. All manufacturers do not rate their amplifiers the same way.

It is possible to calculate the exact continuous average power from any amplifier. Just run a 1000 Hz signal into the amplifier input. Run the input up until the amplifier just starts to clip (distort). Now measure the AC voltage across the output load terminals. Take that voltage, square it, and divide that by the impedance (in ohms) of the output loss (the loudspeaker's impedance in ohms). Suppose you measured 20 volts AC. Squared it would give you 400 watts, but only if there is an output loss of 1 ohm. However, very few amplifiers are loaded with 1-ohm loudspeakers. Most amplifiers are provided with terminals for 4-ohm, 8-ohm or 16-ohm loads.

RMS

RMS stands for Root Mean Squared. RMS power is calculated as:

$$RMS = \frac{(voltage)^2}{load}$$

For the amplifier in the previous example, here are the different results we can get with 20 volt, AC measured continuous power:

$$
\begin{array}{rcl}
4 \text{ ohm load} &=& 100 \text{ watts} \\
8 \text{ ohm load} &=& 50 \text{ watts} \\
16 \text{ ohm load} &=& 25 \text{ watts}
\end{array}
$$

It is easy to see how the power rating values can be manipulated. Many manufacturers will not tell the consumer what values were used to measure the RMS output. Always ask to see specification data before purchasing.

THD

Unwanted harmonics can be added to the original signal, adversely effecting the output of the amplifier. Total harmonic distortion (THD) is measured at rated power levels and usually ranges from about 0.1% to 0.25% of 20 to 20,000 Hz. Intermodulation distortion is measured for combinations of frequencies.

Connection to Mixer/Preamp

The amplifier is normally connected to a mixer or preamplifier by means of a line-level cable and connector. Although your home system may use RCA jacks, pro sound models use an XLR balanced connector. Balanced inputs are around 50 k ohms and unbalanced are around 40 k ohms.

4. Power Amplifiers

Output Impedance and Loading

The amplifier has terminals for attaching loudspeaker cables. Normally there are 4 ohm, 8 ohm and 16 ohm terminals. The amplifier must be loaded with the appropriate loudspeaker impedance. Remember to calculate the change in impedance with series or parallel hookups. For loudspeakers of the same impedance, in series the combined impedance is N (number of loudspeakers) times Y (impedance of one loudspeaker). In parallel, the combined impedance is Y divided by N. For example, two 8-ohm loudspeakers hooked in series have a combined impedance of N x Y = 16 ohms. In parallel, the same two loudspeakers have a combined impedance of Y / N = 4 ohms.

8-Ohm and 70-Volt Systems

An amplifier loaded with an 8-ohm loudspeaker is considered to be a low voltage system. Normally the manufacturer will state the correct working load for the amplifier. This may change depending on whether loudspeakers are switched on and off during a production, or if there are long runs of speaker cable, or if several loudspeakers are connected in series or series-parallel, which generally produces a high impedance load. In those cases a solution can be found by designing a high voltage system to feed the loudspeakers. This type of system is used primarily in auditorium paging applications, or running several speakers to dressing rooms, lobby, greenroom or box office. The loudspeakers are fed at high voltage (70 volts, for example) and transformers are placed to step down the 70 volts to 10 volts or below to feed the loudspeaker itself. For instance, a 40-watt amplifier can be used to feed two 10-watt capacity loudspeakers and four 5-watt loudspeakers with no loss of impedance. This high voltage system has the tremendous advantage of allowing loudspeakers to be switched on and off almost at random without affecting either the amplifier or the remaining loudspeakers.

Damping Factor

Amplifier damping has an effect on the performance of a loudspeaker. An amplifier with a high damping factor can control the motions of a loudspeaker cone better than an amplifier with a low damping factor. The damping factor of an amplifier is expressed as the ratio of loudspeaker impedance to amplifier source impedance. For a loudspeaker of 8-ohms impedance and an amplifier with an internal output impedance of 0.5 ohms, the damping factor is 16. It is important that the impedance seen by the loudspeaker "looking back into" the amplifier should be as low as possible because the loudspeaker cone is springy in its mounting. A large ratio improves the loudspeaker damping. A loudspeaker of 8-ohms impedance "looking back into" an amplifier of 0.16 ohms output impedance will have a damping factor of 50, a significant difference from the previous example. "Looking back into" is an expression used to designate the point from which a circuit is to be considered. The internal output impedance of the amplifier is the actual impedance seen when "looking into" the output terminals of the device. This internal impedance may be only a fraction of the specified load impedance. If a signal corresponding to a single push of the cone is fed to the amplifier, the cone moves forward, but when returning to its rest position it can overshoot and oscillate backwards and forwards for a few cycles. This extends the duration of the sound and is a kind of distortion. It must be kept to a minimum by damping the oscillations with as large a damping factor as possible. The Practicum at the end of this chapter gives an example of how speaker wire can affect the damping factor.

Transistors and Magnetic Fields

Most manufacturers build amplifiers with transistor or MOSFET (metal oxide silicon field effect transistor) technology. The original tube amplifier has given way to transistors, and then to MOSFETs, which are really just solid state tubes, but there have been few major breakthroughs in amplifier design before digital. The basic rule is that an amplifier that

4. Power Amplifiers

can provide super performance specs in the areas of slew rates, damping factor and distortion will be the one for professional operations.

Digital

The advent of digital technology has had a gradual but profound impact on power amplifier manufacturing. Manufacturers of power amps must consider that the digitalization of various audio components has increased performance expectations for their products. Digitalization has enabled pro audio users to decipher imperfections within an audio system, especially amplifier noise. As a result, manufacturers are seeking new ways to lower distortion rates, raise damping factors and eliminate magnetic hum.

Amps are the major link between microphone and speaker. They deal directly with high voltage. Digital technology is forcing every aspect of this process to become better. Previously, all an amp had to do was run a system. With the improvement in other components in the chain, such as signal processors and speakers, the importance of a high-quality amp has increased. Digital logic is used for remote control of settings, trouble shooting, and protection from short circuits and overheating. Problems can be tracked digitally rather than using mechanics to circumvent them. A lot of mechanical methods introduce distortion into the picture.

One path manufacturers are taking to incorporate digital technology into power amps is PWM, a switching technology now being perfected. PWM (pulse width modulation technology), used by class D amplifiers, is employed by amplifiers that interpret sound according to the time lapse between signals of a constant voltage level, instead of relying on variations in the level of voltage.

Ninety-five percent of today's amps are linear, class B amps, which produce a lot of heat. Class A amps are primarily used in audiophile applications. They generate a substantial amount of heat and are too heavy and expensive for touring or most theatre applications. PWM amps will be the wave of the future, but some problems need to be solved first. One problem is that radio interference from these amps tends to disrupt AM radio bands. Another is that the circuitry requires five times as many components. The more parts you have, the greater the possibility of failure. Another problem is the power supply. Current comes from the wall, and this poses a problem until clean digital power supplies can be developed.

4. Power Amplifiers

Practicum

An amplifier has a damping factor of 50 for an 8 ohm load. What is the amplifier output impedance? To solve this problem, use the following formula:

$$\text{Damping Factor} = \frac{\text{Normal Load Impedance}}{\text{Amplifier Output Impedance}}$$

The amplifier output impedance is calculated thusly:

$$50 = \frac{8}{x} \qquad x = \frac{8}{50} \qquad x = .16 \text{ ohms (amp output imp.)}$$

The amp is connected to a speaker by three meters of 22 gauge cable (ordinary two-color speaker cable). What is the total resistance of the cable if it has a resistance of 0.1 ohm/meter?

$$3 \text{ m} \times 0.1 \text{ ohm/m} = 0.3 \text{ ohms}$$

What is the damping factor if you consider the total impedance of amp plus cable?

Total impedance of amp plus cable: 0.3 + .16 = .46

New damping factor: $D = \dfrac{8}{.46} \qquad D = 17.39$

The original damping factor was 50. Now, with ordinary cable, it has degraded to 17.39. What happens to the damping factor if we use 16 gauge lamp cord (zip cord) with a cable resistance of 0.024 ohm/meter? (Assume same length)

New cable impedance: 0.024 x 3 = 0.072 ohms

Impedance of amp plus cable: 0.072 + .16 = .232

Recalculated damping factor: $\dfrac{8}{.232} = 34.48$

5. Loudspeakers

Most loudspeaker systems consist of one or more drivers installed in an enclosure. Figure 10 shows a sectional view of a dynamic cone driver. The driver consists of several parts, most prominent of which is the "diaphragm," the shallow cone or rounded dome that is visible when the enclosure's grille is removed. Attached to the back of the cone or dome is a cylindrical bobbin on which is wound a coil of fine wire, the voice coil. The voice coil fits into a narrow circular slot in an assembly consisting of a permanent magnet and a surrounding

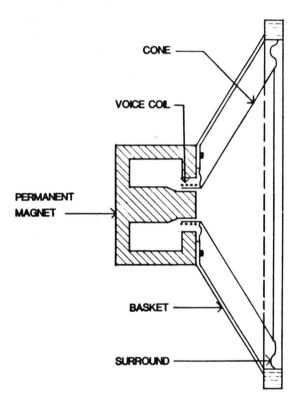

Figure 10. Dynamic cone driver

structure of soft iron. The slot, or "gap," has to be narrow in order to concentrate the magnet's field on the voice coil. A circular piece of spring-like corrugated fabric, called a spider, is used to guide the movement of the voice coil so that it remains centered in the narrow slot of the magnetic assembly. Woofers (low-frequency drivers), tweeters (high-frequency drivers), and mid-ranges are all made this way, though they differ in details. This description applies to "dynamic" loudspeakers, which represent the vast majority of speakers sold today. Electrostatic loudspeakers are constructed differently.

Dynamic Cone Loudspeakers

The combination of voice coil and magnetic assembly constitutes an electric "motor" designed to be driven by the output of an audio amplifier. The amplifier, in sending an audio signal to the speaker system, causes an electrical current to flow in the voice coil—a small current for small signals, a large one for loud musical passages. The flow of the current causes a varying magnetic field to be formed about the voice

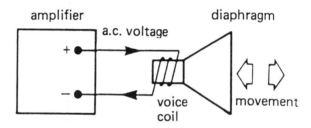

Figure 11. Voltages applied to the voice coil

coil, and this field, because of its interaction with the driver's magnet, causes the coil to move rapidly backward and forward (vibrate) in the magnetic assembly slot. And since the coil is attached directly to the diaphragm, it also moves, in turn imposing its vibratory motion on the air in the form of rapid pressure variations, otherwise known as sound.

The louder the sound a given speaker system is called upon to produce, the greater must be the current flowing through its voice coil and the longer the back-and-forth mo-

5. Loudspeakers

tions (excursions) performed by the voice coil/diaphragm assembly.

Aside from the obvious possibilities of direct physical abuse, like rupturing the diaphragm with a well-placed kick or dropping the whole loudspeaker down a flight of stairs, there are two common sources of loudspeaker damage: excessive voice coil excursion (especially in the woofer) and the buildup of excessive heat in the voice coil (especially in the tweeter).

For most music reproduced at average home loudness levels, the back-and-forth excursion of the voice coil is only a small fraction of an inch. This usually leaves enough excursion in reserve to handle the loudest musical moments on modern recordings, or even to permit a substantial increase in the volume-control setting. But if you ever drive the voice coil beyond its design range, several things can happen. The voice coil may be driven all the way back into the slot in the magnet structure so that it strikes the back plate of the assembly. This voice-coil "bottoming" is quite audible, often taking the form of a rapid clacking or clicking or even a hair-raising "blatt." Another possibility is that excessive excursion will drive the voice coil so far forward that it pops out of its slot and fails to reenter it properly. This often results in permanent misalignment. The voice coil then rubs against the internal parts of the magnet assembly, causing a scraping or rattle on certain notes. Another possibility is that the coil could become jammed in the slot, preventing further movement altogether. Excessive excursion may also stretch or tear the fabric spider that holds the coil centered in the gap, or it may similarly damage the diaphragm where it is bonded to the metal frame of the driver. Finally, there are the wires that carry the electric current to the voice coil from the speaker's input terminals (or from the crossover). If the coil is vibrating back and forth too vigorously, these wires are flexed excessively and may fray and finally break.

When you play music loud, your amplifier puts more electrical current through the voice coils of your speakers.

Whenever an electrical current flows in a wire some heating occurs, and the greater the current the hotter the wire becomes. That is why house wiring is equipped with fuses or circuit breakers to stop excessive current safely before it can overheat the wires in your walls and start a fire. There's not too much danger of fire inside your loudspeakers, but it is possible, by persistently playing music at excessive loudness levels, to build up enough voice-coil heat to melt the insulation of the voice-coil wires thus causing a short circuit, or to char the voice-coil form and the adhesive bonding the wire. Tweeters are particularly susceptible to this kind of damage, since their design requires low-mass voice coils with thin wire that heats up all the more quickly.

Compression Drivers

In a compression driven loudspeaker, the magnetic action is identical to, but the acoustic action is different from, a moving cone loudspeaker. The compression driver creates

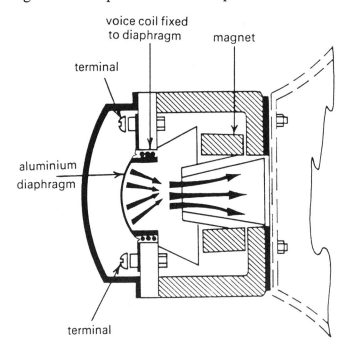

Figure 12. Compression driver

sound pressure waves directly. The thin metal diaphragm of a compression driver acts to compress a volume of air in the pressure chamber. The chamber is vented to the outside by a narrow throat leading into a horn-type radiator. The horn couples the varying pressures in the throat to the air of the room. The compression driver is able to overcome many of the high-frequency break-up problems of the cone driver. Modern compression drivers are able to operate to the upper limits of hearing at very high levels with low distortion.

Subject to the same mechanical and thermal limitations as the cone driver, the compression driver is a more delicate device and will withstand less overload abuse than the typical cone unit. Two great killers of compression drivers are mechanical failure due to excessive power at the low end of its operating range and thermal burnout due to feedback. Compression drivers dislike feedback and low frequencies.

Two major speaker manufacturers, EV and JBL, have designed compression drivers containing neodymium, a highly magnetic material which allows for a decrease in size and weight of the driver and a 1 dB increase in efficiency over comparable ferrite models.

Compression drivers are never used in the bass region. While a few operate as low as 300 Hz, most are rated for use above 500 Hz, and some operate only as super tweeters above 5 kHz.

Electrostatic Loudspeakers

The electrostatic loudspeaker is made up of a heavy metal plate and a very thin, lightweight metal foil separated by an insulating layer. The plates are charged with a very high voltage—positive on one and negative on the other—thus creating an electrostatic potential between the plates. An audio voltage is superimposed on one of the polarizing voltages causing the potential between the plates to vary in step with the audio. As the electrostatic force changes, the thin foil plate will vibrate in step with the changing audio signal. This movement is passed on to the air around the plate, thus creating sound waves. Electrostatic loudspeakers can do an

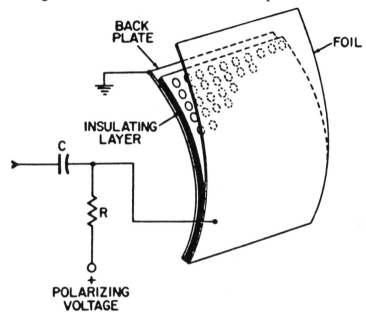

Figure 13. Electrostatic loudspeaker

outstanding job of reproducing the higher sound frequencies, from about 1000 Hz up. They are quite unsatisfactory in bass reproduction since the foil plate cannot make the large movements required to create long wavelengths with useful intensities. These loudspeakers are used as high-frequency units in some very good and expensive home systems. But they are of no use in theatres because they do not have capacity for high volume.

Enclosures

A loudspeaker is an electromechanical device for converting a varying audio voltage into corresponding sound waves. In loudspeaker design, the goals are to limit distortion and to reproduce accurately the audio frequency response of the amplifier. Should it always be flat? Not necessarily. Some loudspeakers have been designed to respond more favorably to certain frequencies than others, such as bass reflex speakers. Loudspeaker enclosures are measured by their resonant frequency, or Q. This refers to the frequencies that the box reproduces best.

Damping of the loudspeaker enclosure is the process of reducing unwanted resonant effects by applying absorbent materials to the surfaces. Successful damping expresses the ability of the cone to stop moving as soon as the electrical input signal ceases. Poor damping allows motion to continue briefly, like an automobile with poor shock absorbers. This hangover creates a "booming" sound in the bass frequencies masking clarity.

The Closed Box

The closed box cabinet may be described as an infinite baffle, because the waves emerging from the back of the cone cannot reach the front of the loudspeaker—they have an infinite path length. These cabinets have a poor low-frequency response.

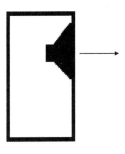

Figure 14. Closed box—infinite baffle

The Vented Box / Bass Reflex

The simplest and best low-bass enclosure is the vented box. The old name for this enclosure is bass reflex. A box of the proper volume is tuned by adjusting the area of the vent to match the needs of the driver. Sometimes it is also necessary to add a duct behind the vent to tune the system. By proper selection of box volume and duct/vent size, a given driver may be operated smoothly to very low bass—say 30 Hz—or it may be made to roll off smoothly at some higher frequency as, for example, in a stage monitor where low bass might cause feedback problems.

Although this concept has been around as long as loudspeakers, there was no reliable mathematical formula for calculating box, vent and duct sizes. It was a matter of experimenting in the workshop until a good combination was found. Failures were so common that most manufacturers for the home market stuck with the closed box which was much easier to get right. Manufacturers of high-power professional equipment used the horn. But Dr. Small and Dr. Thiele from Australia, in a series of articles printed in 1961, and reprinted ten years later in the United States, provided simple-to-use and very reliable formulas to design vented boxes. The vented box is as much as 10 times more efficient (louder) than the sealed box and has a better low-end response. The vented box is not quite as efficient as the horn, but it has a much better low-bass response at a very much smaller size, weight, and cost.

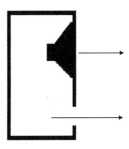

Figure 15. Vented box—bass reflex

5. Loudspeakers

The directional pattern of a cone driver in a vented box is very predictable based upon the dimensions of the box and size of the cone. All bass enclosures are completely nondirectional at low frequencies. Remember that at 50 Hz, the wavelength is 22 feet. It just wraps right around a small box like it wasn't even there. Around 100 to 200 Hz, depending on box size, the directivity begins to narrow down to 160 degrees and holds there up to the frequency whose wavelength is the same as the cone diameter (piston range). At that point, the beam begins to narrow at the rate of 50% per octave.

Multicell Horns

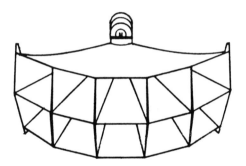

Figure 16. Multicell horns

There are about a half dozen types of high-frequency horns that may be used with a compression driver. The radial horn came first and is the most widely used of all horns. Its biggest problem is that it does not disperse all frequencies equally. As the frequency rises the coverage angle grows progressively narrower. This is called beaming. In an effort to reduce the beaming problem, the multicell horn was created. The multicell is just a group of small horns connected to a common throat. This scheme does not eliminate beaming, it just changes it.

51

Folded Horns

Some horns are being built to operate lower than 150 Hz, but the size gets very large. Remember that mouth size and length determine the low-frequency limits. One way of increasing low-frequency response while maintaining reasonable horn size is to fold the horn. This scheme works well at low frequencies but cannot be used above a few hundred Hertz because the shorter wavelengths begin to distort as they move around the corners.

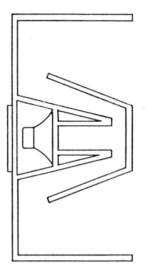

Figure 17. Folded low–frequency horn

An excellent example of the folded horn loudspeaker is provided by Klipsch, one of the leading manufacturers of this type of loudspeaker. The Klipsch La Scala™ is pictured in Figure 18. The cabinet may also be ordered in fiberglass and extruded aluminum for rugged touring demands.

5. Loudspeakers

Figure 18. Klipsch La Scala™ loudspeaker

Resonant Frequency

Drivers are designed and built to reproduce a specific range of frequencies. Thus, there are low, mid and high frequency drivers. The resonant frequency of a driver is determined by hanging the speaker in free air, away from reflecting surfaces. An oscillator is run through a power amp to drive the speaker from 20 to 20,000 Hz. At the resonant frequency, the excursion of the diaphragm will be at its maximum.

Phasing

In loudspeaker systems that use two or more units, it is essential that the diaphragm of each loudspeaker be in acoustic phase with each other. The diaphragms must all move in the same direction at a given instant. When a system is out of phase, it will have a good low-frequency response as well as as

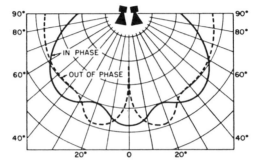

Figure 19. Loudspeaker phase characteristics

a good high-frequency response, but the overall response will be lacking in presence. The phasing can be checked electrically by making sure that the plus and minus terminals of the speaker are wired the same way.

A signal of the same frequency as that of the crossover point can be applied to the input of the system. As the oscillator is moved over a small band of frequencies above and below the crossover frequency, the listener should hear a

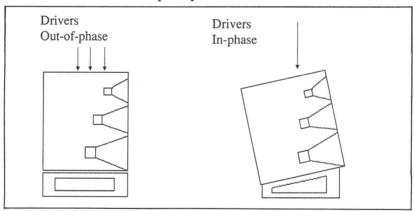

Figure 20. Driver alignment

smooth crossover. If the units are out of phase, a null point will be noted. Figure 19 shows the polar characteristics of two loudspeakers in and out of phase.

It is also possible that alignment of drivers could be the reason for phase cancellation. If the system consists of a multi-cell horn and low-frequency driver it can be improved by moving the horn forward and back until a position is found where a considerable improvement is heard in the quality of reproduction. Figure 20 shows a different situation in which the drivers of a loudspeaker are aligned out of phase. A stand can be constructed to slant the speaker back, bringing the drivers closer to the proper alignment.

Acoustic Coupling

Dr. Amar Bose, professor of electrical engineering at MIT, recognized that it isn't just a speaker's frequency response that determines its sound. He knew that it had something to do with the way sound was projected into the listening room. Theoretical acoustics say that the ideal sound source is a single point radiating sound energy in all directions. Dr. Bose proceeded to design the Bose 901 loudspeaker which utilizes acoustic coupling and direct reflection. The Bose 901s have a unique design which consists of nine identical drivers connected in series. The impedance of each driver is 0.9 ohm. The total impedance is 8.1 ohms. Acoustic coupling refers to the phenomenon that drivers connected in series cannot resonate at the same frequency, so the cones divide the frequencies and reproduce accordingly. Sound projection is from the front and back, eight drivers reflecting off the corner wall surface and one in the front to help imaging and stereo location. The effect is that the listener feels immersed in the music. The Bose system was selected by Calgary for use in the 1988 Winter Olympics.

Crossovers

A crossover is a circuit that divides the signal from an amplifier into frequency bands to feed appropriate loudspeakers, i.e. high frequencies to the tweeter and low frequencies to the woofer. Passive crossovers are merely capacitance circuits; active crossovers are electronic, which may allow frequency and range parameters to be defined or changed.

Hints on Using Loudspeakers

1. Never hook up a speaker when the amplifier is on and being driven by a signal.

2. Avoid feedback: high-frequency compression drivers can very quickly be overpowered by sustained feedback.

3. Always us a DC blocking capacitor on high-frequency compression drivers when bi-amping to protect them from turn-on transients and spurious low-frequency signals.

4. Never turn on low level electronics (mixer, graphic equalizer, etc.) after the power amplifiers are on.

5. Keep dust, dirt, Coca-Cola, beer, popcorn, etc., out of the throat of the high-frequency horn. They present an increased load on the driver and significantly reduce high-frequency output.

6. Avoid ground loops: ground loops and high power amplifiers may be fatal to loudspeakers. Do not make connections to equipment with levels up or power amps on. Use connectors that make ground connections first. Keep cables in good repair.

7. Avoid excessive low-frequency signals as severe cone damage can result. Use high pass filters— 40-60 Hz, 10 dB/octave.

5. Loudspeakers

8. Do not run power amplifiers into clipping as this will reduce both amplifier and speaker life expectancy.

9. A strong grille should be used on floor monitors to prevent foreign objects from piercing the cone. A metal or plastic screen should be used in taverns and cabarets.

10. Casters may help, but when moving heavy speaker cabinets and amp racks, secure them to avoid runaways.

11. A solid support for the speaker system is a necessity. Poorly braced platforms can collapse.

12. Always use a power amplifier with protection against DC voltage at the outputs. Dead output transistors can put the voltage through the voice coil. The power supply current can blow out the voice coil before the fuse has a chance to react.

13. Make a habit of checking the mounting bolts or clamps on speakers for tightness regularly.

14. Avoid excessive equalization. Also, avoid frequency extremes when equalizing as they present demands that most speakers and amplifiers can't handle, especially in live sound reinforcement.

15. Store speakers in areas that maintain fairly even temperature and humidity and not extremes of either.

16. When using a speaker system outdoors keep weather protection handy. Even a small amount of rain or water can damage the bass speaker cone and cause rusting of the internal surface of the drivers.

17. When transporting multicell or fiberglass horns put them into travel cases. It is also advisable to use a hard cover over speakers when transporting them.

18. Always use proper grounding.

19. Use a logical approach when stacking a speaker system and provide a stable structure even at the expense of coverage area.

Practicum

1. Hookup several different types of loudspeakers next to each other and play the same sound through them one at a time. Compare the frequency response by listening to how the speaker reproduces highs, mids and lows. You will be able to judge which of your speakers adds warmth, color and brightness, and which act as low-pass filters. Future decisions on loudspeaker selection and placement will benefit from this type of analysis.

2. Take a damaged loudspeaker, or an old one that is not used anymore, and take it apart. Carefully analyze the driver. Describe and list the parts of the cone assembly including voice coil, magnet, spider and diaphragm.

6. Microphones

Dynamic Microphones

A dynamic microphone has a diaphragm that moves a coil inside a magnetic field to generate an electrical signal. It requires no phantom power and is the most rugged of all.

Moving coil microphone. The most common professional type of dynamic microphone is the moving coil. It operates on the principle that an electrical voltage will be generated in a conductor moving inside a strong magnetic field. Sound pressure waves cause the diaphragm to move. The motion of the diaphragm is passed on to a coil of very fine wire that is centered around a rod of a strong magnet. The first moving coil was introduced by Western Electric in the late 1920s.

Moving ribbon microphone. The moving ribbon operates on the same principle as the moving coil except that here the diaphragm and coil are combined into a single element. They are noted for warm sound and good bass response. A weakness is that they are very fragile. They are great for recording voice (radio narration). After World War II, the RCA 77A ribbon dominated the market in the United States. It was smaller and more portable than a comparable condenser microphone. In 1952, General Eisenhower was entering the race for the presidency. He asked his friend General Sarnoff of RCA for a high-quality microphone that would be small enough not to hide his face. This was the genesis of the RCA Bk-5, the first small ribbon microphone, measuring about one inch in diameter and about six inches in length.

Microphone response curves. Microphones have characteristic response curves and are sensitive to particular ranges of sound. For example, the SM-58 rolls off at 100 Hz and 8,000 Hz. It has a big 6 dB peak around 3,000 Hz to 5,000 Hz. This makes it a dynamite mic for vocals. Figure 21 shows a picture of the most popular vocal microphone in the world.

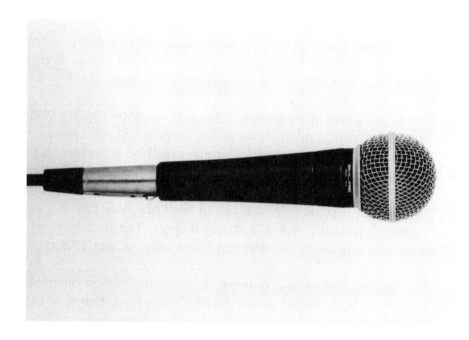

Figure 21. Shure SM-58 (Courtesy Shure Brothers, Inc.)

Condenser Microphones

The first high-quality professional microphone developed was a condenser. It was used in the 1910s as an instrumentation microphone. Its frequency response range is normally from below to above the audible range. It consists of a pair of plates, one or both of which can be diaphragms. The two plates are charged with an electrical potential. When the sound pressure waves cause the diaphragm plate to vibrate, the vibration alters the distance, hence the capacitance, between the two plates, thus allowing a very small electrical current to flow. This feeble current from the condenser plates must be amplified right at the condenser. It is crucial that no more than a few inches separate the plates from the amplifier.

Since the diaphragm is a condenser element, it requires power and electronics. Some types use a battery mounted in the microphone housing. Now it is no problem to build a tiny amplifier no more than an inch in diameter into the case of the microphone. But when they were first used in 1920s and 1930s, the power supply was a large heavy box with the microphone element in one end.

The condenser microphone is more fragile than the dynamic and works well for brass and strings. On-axis response changes in the mid-bass region depending on how close the sound source is to the mic. The difference in bass sounds can be enormous.

Super-cardioid. The supercardioid is manufactured by adding tubes and more rear holes to the chamber. This makes a tighter cardioid pattern with greater back rejection, a reduction in off-axis coloration and a reduction in the proximity effect (see page 65)

Most of the hypercardioid microphones are shotguns with severe off-axis coloration and are often best used only for speech pick-up.

Acoustic cardioid. There is an easy way to make a cardioid with only one element instead of two. It was discovered by accident. At RCA labs a polar response of an omnidirectional mic was found to have a cardioid pattern. The technician had done a poor job of soldering. He had left a small hole in the rear pressure chamber and accidentally created the first acoustical (rather than electrical cardioid).

PZM—Pressure Zone Microphones

A pressure zone microphone consists of a small metal plate upon which is mounted a small block with an XLR connector in one end. The microphone element (a condenser) is less than 1/4" in diameter and is mounted facing the metal plate with only a few thousandths of an inch space between them. There is no such thing as on-axis; all the sounds reaching the PZM will come in along the mounting plate in what is known as the boundary pressure zone.

Sound for the Stage

The PZM is rarely mounted on a mic stand: it goes on the floor, on the ceiling, on a set wall, or attached to the piano lid. Its pickup pattern is hemispherical—one half of an omni. It has no off-axis coloration. A pressure-calibrated electret capsule is mounted parallel to an acoustic boundary and within a very short distance of the boundary. This allows the transducer to operate within the pressure zone formed by the combination of the incident and reflected waves of the boundary. Incident and reflected waves are in phase and do not produce comb filters which are reinforcement and cancellation effects in the response due to phase differences which develop further away from the boundary. By operating in the pressure zone, the PZM does not encounter the comb filters produced by that boundary, and thus can have a smoother response than a free-field microphone, which in most cases will be operated several feet from the nearest boundary. The pressure zone also serves to integrate the direct and random incidence sound fields at the boundary so that the PZM responds to both equally. Free-field microphones display different response curves to the direct and random incidence fields in which they operate, which often produce a result that does not sound natural. PZMs have smooth sounding response and transparent natural sound.

An additional benefit is that the annoying noise characteristic of microphones when accidently rubbed or touched is practically eliminated with the various PZM and tie-bar models. This is due to their small diaphragm mass and the special mounting material which provides isolation between the capsule and the microphone body.

The PCC 160 by Crown is similar to a PZM, but it has a half supercardioid pattern. Current practice has found the phase-coherent electret condenser PCC 160 to be superior to the PZM for floor microphone applications in a musical or review. Three of them can cover an entire 50' proscenium opening.

6. Microphones

Wireless

Wireless microphones of many types are available to reinforce a voice that moves around extensively. A hand-held wireless microphone can be used when the actor or singer wants to move without a cord. If the object is not to see the microphone, a lavalier connected to a transmitter is the answer. This may occasionally present a problem, as in the University of South Florida's production of *The Tempest*, where a nearly-naked Ariel had to have a wireless microphone for a pitch-changed voice. Ultimately, it was taped within his loin cloth.

VHF Synthesized Wireless Microphone Systems supersede the conventional wireless concept. The PLL (Phase Locked Loop) synthesized tuning makes it simple to switch operating frequencies for interference-free operation anywhere. The Sony diversity system uses two transmitter antennae placed apart from each other to simultaneously receive signals of a single wireless microphone or transmitter. The tuner provides two switching control voltages in proportion to the field strength of the incoming signals at each antenna, and comparing these voltages, the tuner automatically selects the stronger input from moment to moment, and delivers it as the output, thus maintaining stable reception with an excellent signal-to-noise ratio. This eliminates antenna dropout and reflection phase cancellation.

The Sony wireless microphone has a built-in limiter and compressor and a frequency range of 30 to 18,000 Hz. The transmitter operates on the 200 MHz VHF band (174.6 MHz to 215.4 MHz) which corresponds to TV channels 7 through 13 in the United States. Channels are allocated in a clever way. Each of the 7 available TV channels is divided into 24 wireless microphone channels with separation of 200 kHz, giving a total of 168 potentially usable channels. The diversity tuner allows pushbutton selection of any of these channels. A signal having wide dynamic range is compressed for transmission on a narrow-band channel and then expanded by the tuner to restore the original signal. Please note that the use of wireless devices is regulated by the Federal Communications Commission and requires an appropriate license.

Caution: The dimming of lights may produce electrical interference over the entire frequency of range of 1 MHz to about 100 MHz. Position the antenna and the wireless microphone or transmitter in a place where such interference is at a minimum.

C-Tape

C-Tape is commonly called a contact microphone. The transducer is a flexible strip of plastic approximately 3 inches wide and either 3 or 8 inches in length. It is sandwiched between two outer layers of plastic. C-Tape is fully flexible and capable of being wound around a pencil. Basically, it is a co-axial transducer with the central element being a flat foil. Around this is wrapped an earthing element. There is a change in capacitance between the inner foil and the outer earthing layer, and the inner foil itself is covered in C-tape's own piezo-electric vinyl—a material like an electret or plastic with a lot of free electron activity in the outer layers. The transducer uses these two effects, the pressure sensitivity on the inner foil and the change in capacitance to convert the sound pressure into electrical signals.

The transducer has the following characteristics:

1. It has a mode of operation that is essentially capacitive but with an electret enhancement.

2. It is a thin tape, 13mm wide, which covers a finite area of the instrument soundboard.

3. It has a density low enough not to significantly damp the vibration surface.

6. Microphones

4. It is totally flexible and will thus conform to the curved body of a violin, double bass or drum shell.

C-Tape was originally designed for use on the drum, where experiment has shown that the closest sound is achieved by its attachment to the inside of the shell.

Phasing

When you speak into a mic, the diaphragm pushes forward and causes a voltage to appear at the connector. The voltage can be either positive or negative, depending on how the connector is wired. If the wires are reversed on pins #2 and 3, and two mics are brought together, the sound will cancel. Take one mic, mark it as a reference, and compare all the rest of the mics to it.

It is best to keep microphones 3 to 4 feet apart when the user is within a 1-foot distance of a microphone.

When placing microphones for a vocalist, instrument or other equipment, place your ear where the microphone is to hear what it is hearing.

Proximity Effect

As the mic is brought within one inch of the program source, it picks up the low frequencies better than highs. This is known as the proximity effect. It's great for a female singer who wants more guts or punch from the PA. All she has to do is bring the mic right up to her lips. Backing off will thin out the tone. But an acoustic guitar is difficult to mic. Low-gain mics must be placed close to the source. When the mic gets into the resonating pattern around the guitar hole, the mic and system feed back at the hole's resonance. Couple this with the proximity effect and the guitar resonates within the low-frequency response range. The problem is now multiplied by the square, not just doubled. In practice, all mics fall short of the ideal, emphasizing some sounds at certain frequencies and limiting others.

Response curves show how the response of the mic has been tailored. Some mics are built with a slight high-frequency boost that adds crispness to the sound. Others may have a switchable bass rolloff, meaning that the bass frequencies will be cut down a bit. A piano needs a mic that is sensitive to the highs and lows of the widest frequency range. A vocal mic will not do a very good job since it is most sensitive in the midrange.

About 40 years ago it was discovered that a boost in the 2,500 Hz to 4,000 Hz range would make a vocalist seem louder and stand out from the backup music without actually being much louder in electrical output. This high-frequency boost is called presence boost. Some microphones are designed with this type of proximity effect built-in.

Omni vs. Uni

An omnidirectional microphone has a sealed chamber behind the diaphragm so that sound pressure can apply force only to the front of the diaphragm. No matter from what direction the sound originates, as the pressure waves pass, the diaphragm will be subject to the push and pull of the varying sound pressures. The advantages of an omnidirectional microphone are:

1. For a given price, an omnidirectional microphone generally has a smoother frequency response than its cardioid counterpart. Such smoothness of response is important because any roughness invites feedback.

2. An omnidirectional microphone is significantly less susceptible to breath pops than its cardioid counterpart.

3. An omnidirectional microphone is significantly less sensitive to mechanical shock than its cardioid counterpart. It is more rugged.

6. Microphones

The first microphones were not very good at the high end. This was the result of a large diaphragm and the large box behind the microphone. A large diaphragm does not operate well at the high frequencies and a large microphone rear housing will cast a shadow in the highs arriving from the rear. Modern omnidirectional microphones have diaphragms less than one inch in diameter and correspondingly small housings.

Cardioid microphones have a highly directional pattern. They are usually more expensive than omnis, but have a significant advantage. These microphones can increase operating distance by a ratio of almost 2:1. This reduces the potential for feedback and is likely to decrease room reverberation and background noise. Cardioids are likely to produce a higher sound level before room feedback, especially when high levels of direct speaker sound reach the microphone from the sides or rear. With a regular omnidirectional microphone, the maximum working distance from the sound source (singer's mouth, guitar, trombone) is about 10 inches; the cardioid microphone will allow the source to be 18 to 20 inches away. It will produce a higher sound level before feedback.

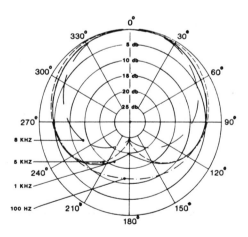

Figure 22. Microphone polar pattern

Sound for the Stage

Polar Pattern

A polar pattern is a graph of the ability a microphone has to pick up sounds originating in a different direction from the principal axis of the mic. Omnidirectional microphones have equal sensitivity to sounds regardless of the direction. Cardioid microphones have unique polar patterns. Refer to Figure 22 for an example. This shows the loss in output (in dB) experienced as a constant-output sound source moves 360 degrees around a fixed microphone at a fixed distance. A unidirectional pattern looks like an apple with the stem at the microphone. An omnidirectional may be represented as an inflated balloon with the microphone at the center.

Microphone Selection and Placement

Microphone selection and placement greatly affects the sound of a recording or live mix. Even if your tape recorder and mixer are the best available, the final result will be poor unless you choose and place the microphones carefully. Each microphone sounds different, and it is important to select the microphone that gives the best sound for a given situation. The frequency response and polar pattern are two of the crucial specifications.

Flat-frequency response mics tend to sound natural. Mics with emphasized high-frequency response sound brighter with more treble. Microphones that roll off below the range of the instrument minimize room rumble. Mics that roll off low frequencies within the range of the instrument tend to sound weak in the bass.

Most condenser mics have an extended high-frequency response, making them suitable for cymbals or other instruments requiring a detailed sound, such as acoustic guitar, strings, piano and voice. Dynamic mics have a response good for drums, guitar amps, horns and woodwinds.

6. Microphones

The polar pattern of a microphone affects the amount of ambience and off-axis sound that the mic will pick up. Omnidirectional mics pick up the most peripheral sounds, unidirectional mics are easier to target. The more ambience that is picked up along with an instrument, and the more an instrument's leakage is picked up by other mics, the more distant that instrument sounds. An omnidirectional mic must be placed closer to an instrument than a unidirectional mic to reproduce the same sense of distance. However, omnis tend to have less handling noise and breath popping than unidirectionals. In addition, the proximity effect bass boost of many unidirectional mics does not occur with omnidirectional. The bass boost may be a desirable effect with tom-toms or vocals.

The number of microphones used in a given situation varies greatly. Many ensembles (such as marching bands, choirs, string quartets) can be recorded using just two mics. An orchestra, a vocal group with many soloists, or a rock band may require multiple microphones for instruments or sections.

When using a hand-held microphone, it is important to use a wind-screen to eliminate explosive breath sounds and keep out saliva. Holding the microphone close to the mouth is a necessity with the ideal position being in front, even with the nose, and pointed down into the mouth. If the actor is at a podium, the usual position is in front of the actor and pointing up toward the mouth as close as possible. Sometimes using two microphones pointed in towards the actor from the sides is efficient. The primary rule in all microphone placement is to get the microphone as close to the source as possible for the cleanest sound and keep the number of microphones to a minimum.

The general rules to avoid feedback are:

1. Minimize the number of microphones. Each additional microphone adds potential for feedback. The choice may be between having a few microphones at high gain or a lot of microphones at a lower gain.

2. Keep microphones as close as possible to the desired sound source. This requires less gain in the mixer and therefore reduces the chance of feedback. Close miking also decreases the amount of leakage.

3. Try to keep sound sources on-axis, especially sources that radiate loudly. Some microphones add off-axis coloration. Boundary mics have almost no off-axis coloration.

4. Keep unused mics off whenever possible. If there is not any sound to be amplified, then it is not necessary to keep the potentiometer up.

5. Use a unidirectional mic whenever possible. It reduces the amount of leakage and is less prone to feedback.

6. When positioning the house speakers, make sure they are downstage of all microphones. Any mic that is pointed toward a speaker will feedback very quickly.

7. Use a direct injection box to mix electronic instruments.

To mic the following:

Vocals - in front of and even with the nose, pointed down into the mouth.

Instrument amplifiers - on short stands aimed directly into the speaker from about 6 inches to a foot away. Also split outputs, sending direct to one channel, mic to another.

Piano - use a PZM placed inside the lid in the center, or on the underside, or use two microphones, one for the high and one for the low end.

Horns - very close to the instrument, if not in the bell of the horn.

6. Microphones

Leslie cabinet - upper part of cabinet to pick up sound of the rotating horn. Usually there is a big open slot at the back. Another mic at the bottom will pick up the bass frequencies.

Synthesizers - direct, or direct injection box.

Choir - mics placed with 3:1 rule. Thus, if mics are 4 feet above the heads, there should be 12 feet of separation between the mics. If placed 6 feet above the heads, there should be 18 feet of separation.

Acoustic guitar - at the center hole with the mic pointing straight at the hole at a distance of about 6 inches. Make allowances for the amount of room needed by the musician to play the guitar. Some acoustic guitars have pickups that allow the use of a direct injection box. This will yield the clean precise sound that is usually wanted with acoustic guitars.

Upright bass - low notes produced by the upright necessitate that the microphones be more sensitive to lower notes. In addition, because the string bass is played with one end resting on the floor, the mic can be attached to a short floor stand about six inches in front and pointed at the bridge or somewhere between the bridge and f-hole.

Woodwinds with reeds - these instruments employ a mouthpiece containing a reed. Most of the sound level escapes through the top five or six finger holes with a little left to radiate from the end of the instrument. Place the microphone either at the finger holes or at the bottom end of the instrument.

Woodwinds without reeds - flutes produce their sound when air is blown into a hole on the mouthpiece. Most of the sound originates near the mouthpiece so placing the mic near the player's mouth will give good results. Another technique is miking the flute approximately a third of the way down the barrel, pointing directly at the instrument from about two inches away.

Sound for the Stage

Kick drum - drums are among the most difficult instruments to mic. The sound of a drum stick hitting a tom-tom or snare may overload a microphone. A good way to mic a kick drum is to remove the front head and place a pillow inside of the shell. This will reduce some of the resonance of the kick, creating a tighter sound with punch. A mic can either be placed directly on the pillow or on a stand facing the shell. Be sure that the chosen mic has good low-end response and is capable of withstanding sharp transients at high SPLs. If the drummer does not wish to remove the front head, try miking the drum from the back (batter or beater) head.

Snare drum and high hat - use a mic placed above the two to pick up both of the instruments. A condenser mic can be pointed downward on top of the cymbals. Snare drums can be miked with dynamic mics on top and bottom.

Mallet instruments - this is an interesting challenge. The ideal is to mic each note on the keyboard, but this is impractical. A microphone about 18" above will work, or use two mics, one each for the high and low ends.

Harp - place the mic on a short floor stand with a gooseneck or boom and point it perpendicular to the sounding board near the middle to low strings. An alternate method uses a small condenser mic wrapped in foam padding and placed in one of the upper holes.

6. Microphones

Practicum

1. Select an assortment of microphones from your inventory, place them on stands and connect them to a mixer that is amplified through loudspeakers and monitor. Speak or sing through each mic in turn to hear what they sound like through the system. Listen for proximity effect and frequency response characteristics.

2. To illustrate the importance of phasing, take two mics, one in each hand. While speaking into one, move the other away and then bring it close. Note that as you bring them closer together, the sound intensifies (provided they are in phase).

3. Unplug the connector of one microphone. Reverse the wires on pins 2 and 3. Plug the mic back in. Repeat the experiment in #2. Notice that as you bring the two mics together the sound will cancel. There is also a response change that happens gradually as you are bringing them together.

7. Turntables and Cartridges

Description

The turntable is one of the most basic components in an audio system. Its duty is to rotate at a selected speed with no fluctuations, and to provide a vibration-free environment for the record. The first sound reproducing devices made by Thomas Edison were hand-cranked cylinders, later replaced by spring-wound phonographs. Most turntables today are driven by electric motors. Electrically driven machines are very accurate devices, with less than 1% deviation in designated speed. The method by which the power from the motor is transferred to the turntable platter classifies the drive mechanism. The three most common types are belt-drive, rim- or idler-driven and direct-drive.

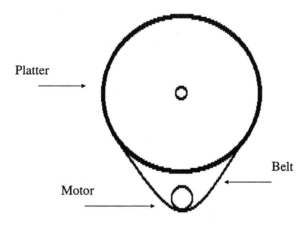

Platter

Belt

Motor

Figure 23. Belt–drive turntable

Figure 23 shows belt-drive turntable with a single motor. The motor is connected to the platter by means of a belt. Speed, measured in revolutions per minute (rpm), is varied by shifting the belt from one pulley to another. In the basic belt drive system, a lever moves the belt across a stepped pulley to change between 45 and 33 1/3 rpm. The disadvantage of the belt-drive system is that the belt may slip or deteriorate.

Figure 24 shows a rim-drive turntable. This type uses a combination of idler wheel and motor to transfer the power to the rim of the platter. This system is not known for high performance and is commonly found on cheap portable phonographs. Many machines designed for children employ the idler, or puck method.

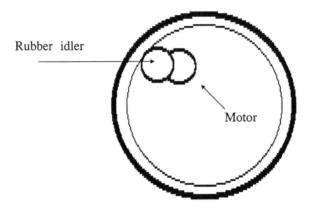

Figure 24. Rim–drive turntable

In a direct-drive turntable the motor drives the shaft directly. The motor, and thus the speed, may be quartz-controlled. This has several advantages. Direct-drive turntables can start fast without hestitation and pitch may be changed by varying the speed. Although direct-drive turntables are quite common, belt-drive units are preferred for demanding applications due to their ability to eliminate low-frequency rumble. However, if you dub records on to tape for dance, you may want the speed variation capability of a direct-drive turntable for precise rhythmic accompaniment.

The tonearm is another component of a turntable system that must be considered. There are two main types, pivoted and tangential. The pivoted tonearm is the most common one, where the tonearm is attached on one side of the platter and pivots to move across the record. The tangential tracking method moves the stylus across the record in a linear fashion.

7. Turntables and Cartridges

Although this seems to be quite modern, it was actually employed by Edison who used a feed screw to track the needle across his original cylinder.

The tonearm must track the groove across the record while supporting the cartridge and stylus at a specific height. Built-in antiskating devices and adjustable counterweights will accomodate different cartridge weights and tracking forces to minimize the friction between stylus and record groove.

As you are well aware, the trend now is towards tape, cassette, compact disc or digital recordings. However, before scrapping the turntable, remember that many classic recordings will never be available on CD. Those old albums and sound effects records may be valuable some day. Keep the turntable, and you can improve its sound simply by obtaining a better cartridge. The best turntables and cartridge assemblies still rival some digital reproduction methods.

The phono cartridge is one of the smallest and, in many ways, the least understood of audio components. Despite its diminutive size, the cartridge performs a seemingly impossible task. When picking up the two channels of a stereo program, the stylus is simultaneously deflected laterally and vertically at frequencies that can exceed 15 kHz, sometimes experiencing accelerations in excess of 30 times the acceleration of gravity. Despite these severe conditions, the stylus must remain in continual contact with the groove walls or blatant distortion will result.

The part of the cartridge that converts the vibrations of the stylus into an output voltage is called the transducer. Many types of transducer systems are available today, each with its own theoretical advantages and disadvantages. Yet designers have discovered ingenious ways to circumvent the problems inherent in each type, and many of them are capable of excellent performance. Regardless of the type of transducer, all high quality cartridges are engineered with the same performance goals in mind: (1) ability to keep the stylus in contact with the groove walls at all times; (2) flat frequency response over the entire audible frequency range; (3) inaudible distortion; (4) a high degree of channel separation; and, (5) output voltage and impedance to match the input characteristics of preamps.

Two basic transducer types are used to generate a pickup's output voltage: magnetic and nonmagnetic. Magnetic transducers, which dominate the market, depend for their operation on changing the magnetic flux that cuts through a wire, generally one that has been formed into a coil. In the other classes are piezolelectric (ceramic), semiconductor, and electret cartridges, none of which use magnets.

The magnetic types are as follows:

Moving Magnet

Also called a fixed coil, moving magnet is the most prevalent type of cartridge. A powerful magnet is fixed to the stylus that vibrates and generates current through adjacent coils. Voltages are induced in both coils of opposite polarity. By connecting them in the proper manner, it is possible to obtain an output voltage twice that of a single coil. Typically this is between 2 mv and 10 mv, a level most preamplifiers are designed to accept. Using two coils greatly reduces hum and noise. These are often called hum-bucking pickups. It is relatively easy to manufacture and replace worn or damaged styli.

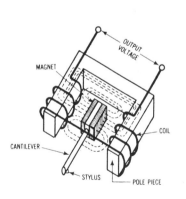

Figure 25. Moving magnet cartridge

A prime example of the moving magnet cartridge is the Shure V15. Pickering, Ortofon, Stanton, Audio Technica, ADC, and Denon all make reasonably priced versions, usually around

7. Turntables and Cartridges

$100, although there are high-end cartridges out there costing more than $1000.

Moving Coil

The operation is similar to the moving magnet, except that the coil is attached to the cantilever and the magnet is stationary. The coil must be as light as possible so that it does not impose an excessive mechanical load on the stylus cantilever (and on the record groove). The output voltage is very small, necessitating delivery to a normal phono input. It is capable of excellent performance often described as spacious with low distortion, but it is often delicate and quirky.

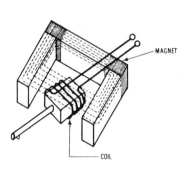

Figure 26. Moving coil cartridge

Since the manufacture requires considerable handiwork, it is moderately expensive. It must be returned to the factory for stylus replacement. Few are available for less than $100. An example of this type of cartridge is the Ortofon Signet MK120HE. It has a diamond stylus, a samarium-cobalt magnet and oxygen-free copper wire.

Moving Iron

Also called variable reluctance, the moving iron cartridge has a fixed magnet and coil. A small piece of iron is bonded to the end of the stylus cantilever and is the part that moves. A gap in the path (air) adds reluctance (similar to resistance, but for magnetic fields) and reduces the amount of flux. The iron moves in the

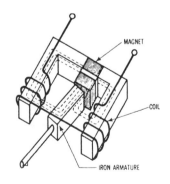

Figure 27. Moving iron cartridge

gap controlling the flux that passes from the permanent magnet to the coils, which are normally connected in a hum-bucking arrangement like that used in the moving magnet cartridge. These are relatively inexpensive to build. It has a large output voltage (large magnet, coil with many turns of wire). The stylus is replaceable by the user.

Ribbon Cartridge

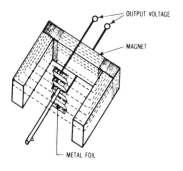

Figure 28. Ribbon cartridge

The ribbon cartridge is similar to the moving coil type. An extremely light, thin piece of metallic foil is attached to the cantilever. The wires form a coil with one loop. It has an output voltage similar to that of a moving coil design. The ribbon cartridge requires a pre-amp and is expensive to manufacture.

8. Compact Discs

Popularity

The compact disc was invented by N.V. Philips, a company with headquarters in the Netherlands. It was first marketed commercially by Sony and has revolutionized the way we listen to music. Compact discs are capable of reproducing sound that seems to emerge from total silence, with a dynamic range in excess of 90 dB. Until DAT (digital audio tape) becomes available to the U.S. consumer, CDs will continue to be the medium of choice for critical listeners.

Sales of compact disc players have rapidly increased, as statistics reveal the following numbers:

1983	45,000 players	$33 million
1984	200,000 players	$104 million
1985	850,000 players	$264 million
1986	1,384,000 players	$357 million

In 1987, retail sales of compact discs reached the $1.5 billion level. As of March, 1988, there were 7 million CD players and 90 million turntables in American homes. But LPs account for less than 10% of the market. Figures for the first half of 1988 show that there were 70.4 million CDs shipped compared with 43.5 million LPs. This is the first time in history that CDs have outsold LPs. Cassette sales are booming, the turntable has become one of the most inactive pieces of hardware around, and CDs are growing in popularity.

How It Works

Refer to Figure 29 below to see how a compact disc is played. The disc itself consists of billions of pits arranged in spiraling tracks. A low-power laser pickup shines a beam through the transparent plastic surface layer of the disc and focuses it on microscopic pits on the information surface. The pits, which represent binary digits (bits) of digitally encoded music, are 0.1 micron deep, 0.5 microns wide, 1.6 microns apart and 1 to 3 microns long. A 3-beam pickup system doesn't actually have three separate lasers, but a single beam of laser light split three ways. The center beam reads the data, while the leading and trailing beams monitor the position in relation to adjacent tracks. This keeps the main beam tracking properly. The laser plays the compact disc from the center of the disc to the outside edges. The revolutions per minute (rpm) change as the laser moves. The disc spins at about 75 rpm near the center and 300 rpm on the outside. As the disc rotates, the laser beam alternately falls onto pits and blanks between them. When the beam strikes a pit, light scatters;

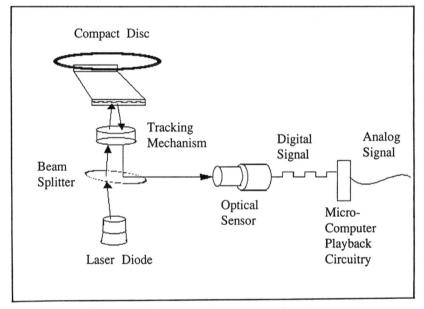

Figure 29. Anatomy of a compact disc player

when the beam strikes a flat surface, light is reflected back to the pickup. Thus a series of pulses is produced and sent to the processing circuits for eventual conversion back to sound.

A CDs digital information is read as a stream of bits which is designed to be sampled 44,100 times per second (a 44.1 kHz sampling rate). The two channels of a compact disc can reproduce frequencies within the 20 Hz to 20 kHz range with a signal-to-noise ratio in excess of 90 dB and total harmonic distortion less than 0.005%. To prevent ultrasonic noise from affecting the audio range of frequencies (below 20,000 Hz), a filter must be used to screen out unwanted signals. Early CD players used analog filters with very steep cutoff slopes. Unfortunately, frequency phase shifting caused by such filters makes a CD player sound harsh, especially noticeable on cymbals, strings and brass instruments.

The latest generation of machines uses advanced digital circuits which filter out unwanted noise before the signal is converted back to analog. A technique called "oversampling" reads the incoming data at two or four times the standard rate, thereby suppressing the frequencies immediately above the audio range. Because oversampling shifts any residual noise to a much higher frequency, a very gentle final filter can then be used after analog conversion.

Because a CD is read as a stream of sequential bits of data, if a portion of the stream is missing or corrupted, so will be the music. Very sophisticated circuitry has been developed so you won't hear the errors. As the stream of data is read, each sample is compared with the one before and the one that follows. Too great a difference between samples indicates an error. By knowing what comes before and after the error, the CD player's brain can interpolate what is missing and fill in the gap. This error correction circuitry is so good even damaged discs can usually be played without degraded sound quality.

Special Features

Excellent sound reproduction is possible with virtually any CD player. A wide range of inexpensive players is available, but there are certain features that will enable you to take advantage of digitally-mastered sound effects and expand the utility of the CD format. Component, rack-mount and portable units may be purchased with many different options. Here are a few things to look for in a CD player:

Specific track number and index number access. A compact disc is usually recorded with music on different tracks. Most players allow access to the tracks in forward or reverse order. Sequential access is convenient only if there are up to 10 or 12 tracks on the CD. However, sound effects libraries may have 80 tracks or more, and there may be individual index numbers for specific effects within a track. The ability to move quickly among the tracks will save a lot of time. The CD player should allow you to skip to individual tracks and index numbers easily.

Wireless remote control. Often CD sound effects are mixed with other recordings to compose a production sound plot. When recording or sampling a CD effect (see Chapter 13) it may not always be practical to have the CD player within easy reach. A wireless remote control will allow you to control input levels or other devices while cueing the CD player on the other side of the room.

Programmable memory. With this feature, tracks on the same disc may be programmed in any order, then cued in that sequence during a production. The pause button should be used to start and stop each cue.

A-B repeat loop. Sometimes it may be necessary to extend an effect beyond the time limit of its original recording. Suppose you need 30 seconds of footsteps and only 10 seconds are available on the CD. A looping feature allows you to select a starting point "A" and an end point "B" anywhere on the program. The designated A-B sector may be played repeatedly until the repeat mode is cancelled.

The optical scanning and digital playback of every CD player result in superior performance, but the technology used in the original recording is an important factor in determining the quality of the sound. The disc is normally provided with information that tells how it was recorded, mixed and mastered. The three types are:

8. Compact Discs

DDD - digital tape used during recording, mixing, editing and mastering.

ADD - analog tape used during recording. Digital tape used during mixing or editing and mastering.

AAD - analog tape used during recording, mixing or editing. Digital used in the mastering process only.

Compact discs should always be held by the edges so the surface does not become clouded with fingerprints. The surface must not be scratched or bent. Do not use record cleaning sprays or static electricity sprays. If the surface is soiled, wipe gently with a soft, damp (water only) cloth. When wiping discs, always move the cloth directly outward from the center of the disc, not in a circular motion as with standard phonograph records. In compact discs, circular scratches along a line of pits are more likely to cause errors than straight scratches across many lines of pits. Handle compact discs with care. Fingerprints, dirt and scratches can cause skipping and distortion.

Manufacture

The disc actually consists of three layers—the disc itself, made of transparent plastic; a reflective aluminum "information surface;" and a lacquer coating for protection. It is on the aluminum information surface that "pits" (physical representations of electronic pulses) are impressed.

Just 300 workers, 100 of them in packaging, produce 50,000 Sony CDs a day. The manufacturing process consists of the following:

Editing. A master tape, one of ten or so in existence, arrives from the recording studio. Three employees spend three to four hours in soundproof rooms editing the tape for digital recording.

Laser Cut. The tape is taken to two workers who create a glass master copy by exposing a glass plate to a laser beam controlled by a computer that reads the digital recording. The laser stores sound by burning tiny pits in the glass surface. These pits—a 10,000th of a millimeter deep—are read as music by compact disc players.

Matrixing. The glass master is put in a plating system to make a metal master and stampers.

Molding. The stampers are placed in injection molding machines. A plastic or high-grade polycarbonate resin is added, and the machine creates—one at a time—thousands of transparent copies of the master. The resulting discs are 1.2 millimeters thick and 120 millimeters wide.

Coating. A very thin (3 to 4 millionths of an inch) layer of aluminum coats the mold's pitted surface. This layer reflects the compact disc player's laser. Then machines add a protective layer of ultraviolet curing resin.

Printing. A few employees run machines that silkscreen labels onto each disc.

Finishing. The discs, stacked on spindles, are packaged automatically in thin, 6-by-12 inch boxes for retail sale.

9. Tape Recorders

Tape Formats

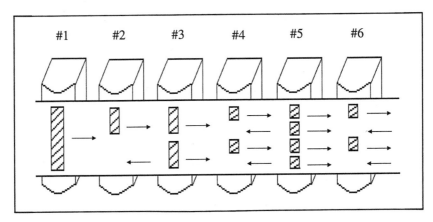

Figure 30. Typical tape formats

Refer to Figure 30 above for examples of six different 1/4" tape formats.

Example 1. Full-track recording: The magnetic flux produced by the head covers almost the whole surface of the tape. The entire tape is recorded in one direction only.

Example 2. Half-track monophonic: The flux pattern generated by the recording head covers less than half of the tape surface and the recording head is off-set to one edge of the tape. A monophonic signal is recorded on one-half of the tape and then the reels are inter-changed and the other half of the tape is recorded. The same half-track head is used for both passes. The tracks are, of course, recorded in opposite directions on the tape.

Example 3. Half-track stereo: Two recording sections (heads) are used to record two tracks simultaneously on the tape. Both channels are recorded in the same direction on one pass through the tape.

Example 4. Quarter-track, 2-channel stereo: Two record heads are used to record all four tracks on the tape. On the first pass through the tape, tracks 1 and 3 are recorded simultaneously. At the end of the first pass, the reels are interchanged and tracks 2 and 4 are recorded using the same two heads that recorded tracks 1 and 3. The actual program on the tape for tracks 1 and 3, and 2 and 4 is recorded in opposite directions, but since the reels are interchanged between passes, the tape is recorded and played in the forward direction for both passes of the tape.

Example 5. Quarter-track, 4-track/4-channel (quadraphonic): The head assembly consists of four separate heads and all four tracks can be recorded at the same time on a single pass through the tape.

Example 6. Quarter-track, single channel (Monophonic): The four tracks on the tape are recorded one track at a time. At the end of each pass through the tape the reels are interchanged and the next track is recorded. The order in which the tracks are recorded is 1, 4, 3 and 2. Four-track recording gives maximum playback time, however, the benefits of stereo reproduction are lost.

Compatibility between various formats are as follows:

1). A half-track mono deck can playback a prerecorded full track tape.

2). A half-track stereo deck can play either a full track or a half-track tape but the signal from a half-track mono tape on side 2 will be played back in the opposite direction. However, the right channel output can be turned down and the left channel only used for playback of both sides of the tape. When playing a full track tape the left and right channel will reproduce the same sounds.

3). A four-track stereo tape deck can play back both 4-track and 2-track tapes and from the point of compatibility has the widest possible range of utilization. When playing a 2-track stereo tape on a 4-track recorder, track #1 will be completely covered by the head. Track #2 will be slightly off alignment; but stereo can still be enjoyed by compensating for the slight loss of track #2 volume with the volume or balance controls of the amplifier. On the other hand, a 4-track tape cannot be played back on a 2-track recorder as both tracks #1 and #2, and #3 and #4 will be reproduced together resulting in mixed unintelligible sounds.

Almost all tape decks are designed and constructed to record and play back only one of the standard formats. A few 4-channel decks have a selectable 2-track playback head for compatibility with prerecorded 2-track tapes. Full-track and half-track monophonic decks for home use are rarely, if ever, available today. Full-track professional decks may be purchased, however.

The gap between heads on multiple track recorders determines the highest frequency that can be recorded. For example, if the head gap is 0.00025 inches, then divide the tape speed (e.g. 7.5 IPS) by the head gap to determine the frequency:

$$7.5 / 0.00025 = 30,000 \text{ Hz}$$

Tape and Speed

Tape speed is measured in inches per second (IPS), referring to how fast the tape travels across the heads. Tape decks like the Otari MX 5050 have two speeds, 15 IPS and 7.5 IPS. Lower-end decks like the TEAC also may have two speeds, but in a lower range, 7.5 IPS and 3.75 IPS. Optimum performance is obtained at the higher speed. Noise reduction systems such as dbx type 1 are designed for use with 15 IPS decks.

The length of a full reel of recording tape, as well as the recording time, is determined by the reel diameter and the thickness of the base material. Running times for various speeds and lengths are listed on the back of most tape boxes.

Polyester base tape is preferred for use in humid or extremely dry areas. The use of 1 or 1/2 mil base tape is recommended for 4-track recording.

Record, Play, Erase Heads

Earlier models of tape recorders used a combined record/play head. With such a head, you cannot record and reproduce at the same time. Another disadvantage of the combined head was in the design of the width of the head gap. Modern head technology generally dictates that the gap width should be different between the record and playback functions for optimum output and frequency response.

When there are severe space and cost limitations, combined record/play heads are still used today. Open reel decks which normally have no head space limitations and usually command a higher price due to their special capabilities, normally have separate Record and Play heads. The separate heads allow monitoring of the tape during recording. This system has distinct advantages. You can verify that your tape is actually being recorded properly as you record. The playback signal can also be connected to the record head for special effects, such as sound-on-sound (simul-sync or self-sync), echo and sound-with-sound.

With separate record and playback heads there will be a time delay between the two heads and the tape speed. For instance, if the record and playback heads are 1 7/8" apart and the tape speed is 3 3/4 IPS, the delay is about 1/2 second. With the tape speed increased to 7 1/2 IPS, the delay is 1/4 second. At 15 IPS, the delay is about 1/8 second.

For some recording situations, even this fraction of a second is not acceptable. If a musician wants to add a new instrument or voice to a song already recorded and wants to listen to the recorded song for timing and synchronization, this delay would present a problem.

9. Tape Recorders

The erase head is located to the left of the record head in the deck. Its function is to purge the tracks of all previous recording by means of a strong alternating magnetic field immediately before the tape reaches the record head. This is done automatically whenever you select record mode in the deck.

Bulk erasure. This is the only satisfactory way to erase previously recorded 1/2 or full track tape to prevent undesirable "cross-talk" or chatter from the former material.

Bias and Equalization

In order to get the magnetic particles on a tape to respond properly to the changing signal supplied to the record head, a preconditioning bias is needed. Most home recorders today use an alternating current (AC) bias at a frequency of 50 to 150 kHz. This bias raises the magnetic level of the oxide particles so that even small changes in the signal from the record head will cause relatively similar changes in the magnetic level of the particles on the tape. Without this bias preconditioning, the oxide particles do not respond properly to the signal from the record head. This high-frequency bias signal is applied to the tape together with the desired audio signal by the record head. Since the bias signal frequency is much higher than the audio frequency range, there is little chance that the bias signal will interfere with the sound reproduction.

The amount of bias (bias level) affects the signal-to-noise ratio, distortion and the frequency response of the tape and hence of the deck itself. Too little bias will allow more distortion than is necessary. Bias also affects the output level of the tape. Normally, as bias is increased the signal level of the tape increases, up to a maximum output level which depends on the type and quality of the tape. Increasing the bias level beyond this point causes the output level (and consequently the S/N ratio) to decrease. The optimum level of bias is usually a compromise between the best results in S/N ratio, distortion, and high frequency response, and usually differs with different types and brands of tape.

The EQ selection must also match the type of tape formulation being used. If a deck was factory-adjusted for standard tapes and the recordist decided to use low noise/high output tapes with their accompanying high-frequency emphasis, the high frequencies would sound too bright. Most tape decks have a switch that can be adjusted to accommodate different types of tape, bias and equalization settings.

Simul-sync

Simul-sync, also known as sound-on-sound or selective reproduction, refers to using the record head to monitor the reproduced program. This enables a recording to be made on another channel synchronized (in phase) with the channel being reproduced. Since the exact sequence of selecting the simul-sync mode is peculiar to each tape deck, it is advisable to refer to the manual of the tape player before proceeding. Recording multiple channel synchronized material, like overdubbing sound effects onto a narrative poem or timing of instrumentals with rhythm sections, is made possible with simul-sync recording.

Time-code

Signals may be recorded on the tape to synchronize two tape recorders, or a recorder and another device like a video recorder (VCR). The Society for Motion Picture and Television Engineers (SMPTE) pioneered the use of a standardized timing reference in the film industry. A camera's film transport is locked by virtue of sprockets, but a time-code is needed to be able to synchronize video and audio tape to film and to one another. The most common is the LTC, or longitudinal time-code, placed as an audio signal on a spare audio track. In the synchronization process, a 1200 Hz modulated square wave is recorded onto a track using a time-code generator. A specially designed device or even a CD player may be used as a time-code generator. The code goes by the acronym of the Society (pronounced as "simp-tee"). There are different types of SMPTE signals depending on how many frames per second are used—24, 25, 30 and drop-frame.

A time-code reader is used to decode the information on the tape and display the data on a frame-accurate digital clock. A time-code synchronizer listens to the SMPTE data recorded on two or more machines, compares the time-code and adjusts the tape speed based upon the results of that comparison. The recorders are locked together by varying the speed of the motors. One of the machines is designated as the "master," the other is designated as the "slave." Its speed is continuously adjusted to maintain the desired relationship. These devices are connected to the tape decks by multipin cables.

The European standard time-code is called EBU and is a 25-frame signal. There is also a time-code for MIDI (see Chapter 13), called MIDI Time Code (MTC). SMPTE-to-MTC and MTC conversion devices are available.

Mechanical Tape Transport Mechanism

Figure 31 provides a typical example of the tape transport mechanism for the Otari MX 5050. It shows in basic diagram how the tape is threaded through the tape guides, across the heads, between the capstan and pinchwheel and around the tension arm. The mechanism for moving the tape incorporates two induction motors for the tape reels and a dc servo motor (direct drive) for the capstan. The capstan works in conjunction with the pinchwheel to move the tape across the heads. A pitch control is available to adjust the control range of the tape speed within $\pm$ 7%. The transport accomodates tape reels of 10 1/2 , 8, 7, and 5 inches in diameter in NAB or EIA hub configurations. In addition to the editing controls, a tape-splicing block is mounted on the head cover. Momentary-contact pushbutton switches on the transport are used to select operational modes: record, play, stop, rewind, fast forward, and edit. All of these modes except edit can be controlled from a remote location using an optional remote control unit.

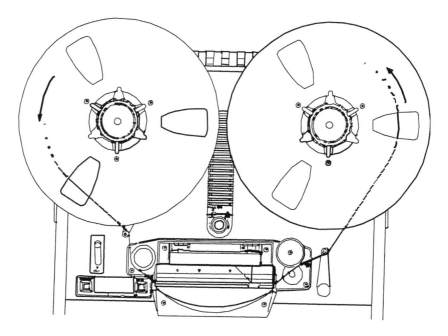

Figure 31. Tape transport mechanism

Demagnetizing and Head Cleaning

The single most important point in tape deck maintenance is frequent and proper cleaning of the heads. The heads should always be cleaned before making important recordings and at least once for every eight hours of use. Dirty heads will cause a reduction in high-frequency response, irregular head wear, drop-outs and occasionally may cause the deck not to record at all. The small amount of time and effort required will be more than compensated for by the higher quality of recording and reproduction available if these procedures are followed.

Commonly used cleaning fluids are chlorothane, hydrogen peroxide and isopropyl alcohol. Be careful with these fluids since they may damage or corrode the head if not used properly. Some advise against strong solvents preferring instead to use a diluted mixture. Using a stiff cotton swab or a foam rubber wand, rub the entire head surface, being cautious not to scratch it. Repeat the process on each head until all discoloration and tape oxides are removed. Clean all metal parts over which the tape passes, such as capstan shaft, tape guides, tape lifters, etc.

During long periods of use, the heads may become slightly magnetized. As a result, high-frequency response will decrease, noise will develop, or in extreme cases, the high frequencies will dropout and noise will be introduced into the tapes. To keep the original fidelity, the heads should be degaussed (demagnetized) at least once for every fifty hours of use. Places specified for degaussing include each head, capstan shaft and guide post. Before proceeding with the following steps, move all prerecorded tapes sufficiently away from the degaussing area.

1. Turn off power to the deck.

2. Turn on the demagnetizer device, bring the tip close to the head and slowly move it up and down four or five times.

3. Slowly move it away from the head.

4. After finishing all points, turn off power to the demagnetizer only after it has been drawn at least twelve inches away from the heads.

Tape Storage and Handling

During playback, the biggest danger to the recording is a magnetized or dirty point on the deck, such as a head or capstan. Care for the tape must be continued even after playing by following these guidelines:

1. Protect the tape from dust. Keep it in the plastic bag in the original carton.

2. Protect the tape from heat. Do not place it on top of audio components. Store it in a cool room but avoid freezing temperatures. Keep it out of direct sunlight.

3. Protect the tape from stress. Tremendous pressure is built up on the inner windings of tape. This pressure is acceptable unless you apply additional stress by bending or squeezing the sides of the reels. The problem is increased if the windings are irregular. Frequent starts and stops will cause uneven winding pressure and the tape will be unevenly wound from side to side within the reel. Slight pressure on the sides will then break or crack the edge of the tape. Therefore, always prepare your tapes for longterm storage by rewinding them using the forward or reverse operating speeds. The fast forward and rewind speeds normally apply a greater tape tension that is not recommended for tapes that will be unused for a time.

4. Protect the tape from strong magnetic fields. Just as a bulk eraser will remove the recorded material, so will a permanent magnet or the voice coil of a speaker destroy your favorite recording.

5. Protect the tape from humidity. Fungus growths will cause irreparable damage to the tape if stored in damp places. Keep the tape in the original plastic bag, but insure that it is dry before storing.

Digital Audio Tape

Digital Audio Tape (DAT) represents the latest advance in electronic sound recording and reproduction. It utilizes ultra-fine metallic pigments developed specifically for helical-scan recording, similar to the recording process in video decks. DAT is available in 40, 60, 90 and 120 minute cassettes. DAT has a dynamic range of 96 dB and an absolutely flat-frequency response from 2 Hz to 20 kHz. The signal is recorded in digital form at a sampling rate of either 44.1 kHz or 48 kHz.

9. Tape Recorders

If a CD player provides a digital output in addition to the analog line output, it is possible to make an exact digital-to-digital recording from the CD to the digital audio recorder, provided that the sampling rates are identical.

Legislation had been proposed by large record companies to restrict digital audio tape recorders. It would have required an anticopy chip developed by CBS to be inserted into every DAT recorder sold in the United States. Its purpose was to prevent the making of digital tape copies from compact discs. Manufacturers were withholding DAT from the U.S. market, believing that the device would hurt the quality of the product. A report from the National Bureau of Standards supports this opinion. Critical listeners had perceived a change of tone in selected passages of music. This was attributed to phase shift in a key frequency, a phenomenon largely confined to piccolos and glockenspiels. David Ranada, technical editor of *High Fidelity*, found evidence of impaired reproduction. A sustained note in the last chord of the cantata in Prokofiev's *Alexander Nevsky*, after the Battle on the Ice and the rout of the Teutons, revealed flaws when played back on a protected DAT. Now all legislative efforts to put the system in DAT recorders have been curtailed.

Panasonic has a pair of professional machines available. The portable SV-250 for field and location recording, and the rack-mount SV-3500 for studio and permanent applications. The portable DAT weighs just 3.5 pounds, has an internal battery, mic/line inputs and 64-times oversampling digital filters. The studio version has high-speed search, full programming functions, multiple repeat mode, XLR ins/outs and a CD/DAT digital interface.

DAT holds the promise of noiseless recordings, sound effects emerging from total silence and instant access of recorded material. These machines may become commonplace in the theatre of tomorrow.

10. Cues and Editing

Designing the Sound Plot

The process of creating a sound cue sheet involves a lot of planning and preparation. The first step is to obtain a script if there is one. Read through the script a couple of times and note what sounds are called for by the Playwright. Then, consult with the Director to understand his concept for the production. At this point, you may have some ideas and be able to make suggestions about environmental or atmospheric sounds, pre- or post-performance music for the audience, and any special effects. Make an input list of all of the sources to be used during the actual production such as tape players, turntables, compact disc players, microphones, cartridge machines or synthesizers. Before loading the show into the theatre, you must confer with the Scene Designer about loudspeaker placement and any on-stage practicals like a radio or phonograph. The Costume Designer also needs to know about any special requirements concerning wireless microphones, transmitters or battery packs. You must also work closely with the Stage Manager to determine where cues will be called during the show. It is important to call sound cues clearly and not confuse them with lighting or fly cues.

The preliminary sound plot will list all of the sound cues, but the actual levels and EQ will have to wait until technical rehearsal. This will also be the time when the cues are coordinated with specific lines or stage business. The final cues must be written in such a way that you can follow them at a glance, without having to read a lengthy narrative. Letters and arrows are the easiest to see. Refer to Appendix E for an example of a cue sheet.

Keep all cue sheets stored with the show tapes. If it becomes necessary, someone should be able to run the show even if the original operator is unable to be present for a performance. Never keep cue sheets or tapes in your car, bookbag or at home during the run of a show. Find a locked cabinet to secure these materials at the theatre.

Leader and Splicing

Editing tape is a way to make creative recordings by eliminating and joining different segments of a recording into one tape. Broken tape can also be easily mended by splicing, one of the steps required in editing. Leader, which is blank noiseless tape, may also be inserted to obtain timed spaces and clean leads into a cue.

Leader tape comes in paper or plastic form. Both are supplied on spools, 1000 feet for paper, 1500 feet for plastic. The 1/4"-width paper leader is 2.5 mil thick, plastic is available in the same thickness as the tape itself, usually around 1 mil. There are advantages and disadvantages to using either type. Plastic leader may not break as easily, but it may stretch if it is put under the stress of fast stops and starts. Plastic leader is easier to work with, and is often marked at 7 1/2" intervals. It is a simple task to insert 5 seconds of silence. You just have to count off five marked intervals if your tape is running at 7.5 IPS.

The first step in the editing process is to precisely locate the section of tape to be removed. On some tape decks that can be done by manually cueing the tape. Mark the tape carefully and avoid getting ink or wax on the heads or transport mechanism of the tape player.

Next, use an editing block and a demagnetized razor blade to cut the tape at the places marked.

Warning: Editing will destroy or seriously cut any material recorded on the other side of the tape. If editing is anticipated, record on only one side of the tape.

Then, perform the following steps using splicing tape or edit tabs. (Never use cellophane tape [scotch tape], which will cause disastrous results as the adhesive will spread and contaminate the heads.)

10. Cues and Editing

1. Overlap the ends to be spliced by approximately 1/2 inch and align them carefully.

2. Cut through the center of the overlapped area at a 45- to 60-degree angle. Many splicing blocks will have grooves to guide this cut.

3. Butt the slanted ends of the cut tape together. Use a straightedge or ruler to assure a perfectly straight alignment.

4. Apply splicing tape to the base side of the tape (opposite to the tape side that touches the head).

5. Place the spliced connection on a hard surface and rub the splicing tape briskly with your fingernail or other hard smooth object. This is to assure a firm adherence to the splicing tape.

6. Trim off the excess splicing tape. You may cut slightly into the recording tape to insure complete removal of the excess. Edit tabs, available from Edit All, eliminate the need to cut splicing tape. The tab can be lifted from it's backing sheet, placed on the splice, and then rubbed with a fingernail. The acetate carrier can be peeled back, leaving the splice attached. This permanent splice may be stronger than the tape itself.

7. When attaching blank leader tape onto your tapes, follow the same procedures given here for splicing.

Practicum

1. Record about twenty seconds of a single tone onto a tape. Then cut and splice the tape at about the 10 second mark. Play back the spliced tape, listening for any "pop" or "click" sound when tracking over the cut that indicates a poor splice.

2. Select a poem or section of a play. Design and record sound effects to go along with a narration. Sound effects may be spliced and recorded on a track separate from the narrative. Some suggested material: *The Shooting of Dan McGrew* by Robert Service, or *Mrs. Murgatroyd's Dime*, a radio play. The former has cold winds, honky-tonk piano and gunshots; the latter has opportunities for pitch change, such as when the dime is put into someone's pocket, footsteps and explosions.

11. Reinforcement

Permanent and Portable Equipment

Mixers, microphones, loudspeakers, amplifiers, cartridge players, tape recorders, compact disc players, digital effects generators, equalizers, noise gates, harmonizers, reverb units, limiters and compressors are all eminently portable these days. Witness the quality and quantity of equipment touring into your local rock music venue. In the past, most of this gear would be available only in permanent studio settings. Today, a typical theatre is likely to have a full complement of touring gear as well as permanent playback and reinforcement equipment.

Mixing boards are appearing on the main floor of the auditorium among the last rows of orchestra seating. Often seats are removed expressly for this purpose. The necessity for the sound operator to hear the sound being mixed is crucial. For a live sound mix, the sound engineer should not be housed in a booth alongside the light board operator. While it is easy for the master electrician to see the effect of his work on the stage through a window, the sound operator must be exposed to the acoustical properties of the hall to do an appropriate mix, especially for live sound reinforcement.

The ultimate touring system these days most likely belongs to a "heavy metal" rock n' roll band. The PA system may fill several semi-trailers with as much as 25 tons of equipment including 200 sound cabinets. The 40,000 watts of such systems may be twice as powerful, per person, in a 10,000 seat arena than your average home stereo system. Monitor systems more powerful than main systems of a few years ago are designed specifically for band members to hear themselves play. The benefit to the theatre sound designer is that a substantial amount of equipment has evolved through the demands of the touring rock n' roll road show.

Sound for the Stage

Microphone and Loudspeaker Placement

One of the problems with loudspeaker placement which has developed in concert situations, both indoors and outdoors, is the proliferation of foldback speakers for the performers. Often there are as many speakers provided for them as for the audience. Microphones will pick up all of this ambient sound unless properly positioned. To avoid having undesirable sound arriving at the mic and distorting the intended sound, it is important to use microphones with highly directional polar patterns.

Control of the stage monitor system is accomplished by providing a separate mixing console. Each musician may then control balance and EQ. The monitor sound engineer is able to listen to each musician's mix on his headphones using the PFL (pre-fade listen).

A typical main mixing console in an auditorium or theatre has between 16 and 48 input channels with 4 to 16 outputs and 6 to 8 effects sends. In an outdoor situation, the console would be located up to 100 yards from the stage. Large performing venues have more complex mixing systems with separate main and enhancement subgroups. Often vocals, effects and music are mixed via subgroups, then routed to stereo mains.

Singing, Instruments and Speech

Musicals and concerts require a big sound that modern audiences have come to expect. Composers, knowing that portable sound reinforcement equipment is as sophisticated and as readily available as that in a sound studio, write orchestrations to take advantage of the new technology. They are unfortunately encouraged by producers who equate loudness with excitement. As a result, actors may lose the ability to project because they rely on sound reinforcement too much to reach the back of the theatre.

11. Reinforcement

Fundamental frequencies for intelligibility are from 500 to 5,000 Hz. Fundamental frequencies for singing range are as follows: bass, 75–340 Hz; baritone, 90–380 Hz; tenor, 130–480 Hz; alto, 190–640 Hz; soprano, 240–1,000 Hz. With a loud band behind the singer these frequencies can easily be overshadowed by the sound arriving from the instruments. Highly directional microphones like the Shure SM-85 or SM-58, have a roll off at 100 Hz and 8,000 Hz and a 6 dB peak somewhere between 3,000 Hz and 5,000 Hz which make them good vocal microphones.

Vocals are almost always split from the instruments so that the loudspeakers used for vocals can be equalized to fit the requirements of the singer. The instruments can then be routed to their loudspeakers. This isn't always practical in a small theatre where loudspeakers are not as plentiful.

Electronic instruments may be routed to the mixer through a direct injection box. Since this eliminates the need for a microphone, there is no off-axis sound to worry about. Instrument amplifiers sometimes have an output sufficient to go directly into the mixer. Synthesizers, electric organs and guitars can use the direct injection box. Microphone inserts are also available for certain wind instruments, such as the flute.

In establishing the overall sound for instrument reinforcement, begin with the individual instruments and then the individual sections of the band or orchestra. Do the strings, brass, woodwinds, drums and percussion sections and then move on to the solo instruments, then the backup vocals and finally the lead vocalist(s). Clarity, articulation and balance are the objectives.

Use the rehearsal period to get rid of all feedback and set the proper levels. Try not to ride the fader except during the rehearsal period. Major changes should be noted on the sound plot or cue sheet. The essence of proper sound balancing is to use your ears and follow the sound plot. Do not over EQ. Begin flat and adjust only as necessary.

Psychoacoustics

Acoustics refers to the science of sound dealing with the propagation and transmission of sound waves. Acoustics describes the effect of various mediums, including reflection, refraction, diffraction, absorption, and interference, as well as the characteristics of rooms, theatres and studios. The elements and properties of acoustics are considered in greater detail in Chapter 14.

Psychoacoustics also considers human perception of sound. It begins with the ear and the process of using sensory apparatus to perceive or hear sound. Thus, it is necessary to consider not only the physical environment in which the sound is generated, but the location and predisposition of the listener. A good example of psychoacoustics in action is the loudspeaker demonstration room of your local audiophile store. The environment is usually well designed from the standpoint of comfort and listening pleasure, with on-axis directivity, well placed reflective surfaces and relaxing chairs or couches for the customer. This contrived environment may color your perception so that when the selected speaker is taken home to an apartment with linoleum, plaster, glass and beanbag chairs it sounds completely different.

The object of theatre acoustics is to project the sound of the performance out to the entire audience and to have it arrive everywhere with similar characteristics of spectrum and intensity and without excessive reverberance. The purpose of a sound reinforcement system is to present amplified but natural sound. Placement of the sound source may be anywhere on stage with the sound waves arriving at the listener's ears at different rates and from various paths. The stage and auditorium will absorb or reflect sound according to the architectural elements that are present. Since sound reflects around an enclosed environment until it is absorbed,

or decays through loss of energy, the "hard" and "soft" surfaces play a big part in acoustics. Theatres for live stage performances are "live" or have a lot of hard surface area which
reflects sound to overcome the absorbing qualities of a seated
audience. Cinemas are designed to reproduce sound through
loudspeakers, so they may have many "soft" surfaces. Each
auditorium will have its own acoustic characteristics.

As in lighting, the angle of incidence of the sound wave
equals the angle of reflection. Loudspeakers that coincide
with the resonant qualities of the hall can double the range of
frequencies. Noise from sources like air conditioning, stage
motors, lobbies, rehearsal rooms, and greenrooms are considered undesirable masking noises and can interfere with the
purity of sound in the performance space. Sound from traffic,
aircraft, emergency sirens can also be annoying. Lower Sproul
Plaza on the campus of the University of California at
Berkeley is a place where percussionists enjoy practicing due
to the excellent reverberant quality of the concrete and buildings. Zellerbach Auditorium, an excellent facility for most
large touring shows, faces the same plaza. At least one performance of Marcel Marceau has been delayed due to intermittent noise leaking through to the audience and stage.

12. Signal Processing and Effects

Noise Reduction

Professional components that increase the dynamic range and reduce the noise of the medium (tape, for instance) have substantially improved the quality of sound in the theatre. The first effective noise reduction was developed by Ray Dolby primarily for tape recording. The Dolby system requires that the tape carry a reference tone for adjusting the threshold of the circuit. In playback this reference tone is used to set the playback level. The Dolby system scans the audio program and increases the volume of the passages and sounds that are identified. Dolby-encoded and expanded material stands out clearly from the background. There are three types of Dolby noise reduction. Dolby A is used for professional applications, Dolby B has been modified to raise the headroom, and Dolby C was developed to increase the effect of noise reduction.

Where Dolby is a dynamic system, dbx differs from Dolby in that it is not frequency or dynamic range sensitive. It is a compander system, compressing the program during recording and expanding during playback. The dbx Model 911 is a typical example. It uses dbx Type I noise reduction for professional quality tape recorders. It doubles the dynamic range of the transmission medium to greater than 115 dB. Depending on the individual channel noise of the medium, it can reduce the noise of the medium 40 dB or more. This is achieved by compressing (encoding) the signal at a 2:1 ratio and applying a carefully tailored frequency response pre-emphasis during recording, and then expanding (decoding) the signal at a 1:2 ratio with a precisely complementary deemphasis during playback. The companding is linear over a 100 dB range and requires no pilot tones or special calibration.

Type I is to be used only on tape machines with flat-frequency response ($\pm$ 1 dB from 20 Hz to 20 kHz) and running at 15 IPS or greater, with full headroom maintained at high frequencies. Type II was developed for media where the high-frequency response is not as flat and headroom is reduced because of tape saturation or other reasons. The two systems are incompatible because the filters and pre-emphasis used in the rms detectors are different.

The benefit of the 2:1 ratio compression is that the signal becomes easier for any medium to handle. Its dynamic range has been cut in half, with the hottest levels considerably reduced and the softest passages boosted. On decoding, the signal is precisely expanded back, and the original dynamic range of the program is retrieved without hiss, saturation distortion, or degradation of frequency response. There is none of the noise buildup normally encountered in transferring information from one recorded medium to another. Noise present in the original, naturally, is not reduced in this process.

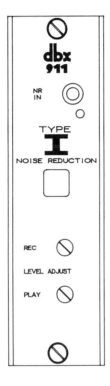

Figure 32. dbx 911 Type I Noise Reduction Unit

Although simple in theory, classic 2:1:2-compander noise reduction could not be achieved before the development by dbx in the early 1970s of two patented circuits, the Blackmer rms detector and the voltage-controlled amplifier (VCA). The former enables optimum decode tracking and transient response despite the phase shifts typically induced by tape recorders. The latter affords precise gain control over an extremely wide dynamic range while maintaining very low noise and distortion.

With today's hotter tapes and faster meters, there are no longer any hard and fast numbers about maximum recording

12. Signal Processing and Effects

levels with dbx noise reduction. Generally, recording levels should always be as high as is consistent with clean sound. This means that peaks almost invariably should go well above the decks's nominal 0. In some cases peaks may go above +3, the end of the meter range for many decks, depending on the dynamic range and the spectrum of the program material. Synthesizer, female chorus, brass, percussion, music with considerable high-frequency energy, transients, and the greatest peak-to-average ratios, will require close attention to the meters and more prudent settings. But electric guitar, chamber music and small-ensemble jazz, piano, strings, male vocals, and any material that has been limited or compressed beforehand may usually be put on the tape at healthy, high levels.

Don't forget to mark the tapes "Encoded with dbx I," or "Encoded with Dolby A," since undecoded playback of encoded tapes or decoded playback of unencoded tapes is not much fun.

Digital Reverb and Delay

Early versions of digital delay, such as on 60's recordings of the Beatles, used tape loops. You can hear a primitive form of digital delay by recording two identical tracks on a tape recorder, playing them back using the normal playback (reproduce) head for one channel and the record head as a reproduce head for the other channel. You can use the record head as a playback head if your tape recorder has a self-sync or simul-sync function. What you will hear is one track played through the record head and the other played through the reproduce head which may be more than an inch away. Depending on tape speed, that gap can create a substantial delay to your ears.

Another place where delay occurs is in the large concert hall. Remember that sound takes exactly one second to travel 1130 feet. Outdoor stadium shows must use digital delays for the speaker towers at the back, so that the audience does not experience unintelligible delay from the stage.

A typical example of digital delay is the Industrial Research DF-4015 Audio Signal Delay. This device is a compact unit intended for delaying high quality audio signals. A principle application is time-of-arrival synchronization of loudspeaker signals in sound reinforcement systems. Four models provide one, two, three or four outputs. Each output is independently adjustable in 3 millisecond steps to 192 milliseconds maximum via thumbwheel switches. True digital processing, using RAM for delay, maintains signal fidelity independent of delay setting. The DF-4015 has a 90 dB dynamic range, 15 kHz bandwidth, and level setting LEDs.

Compressors/Limiters

Dynamic range is the difference in dB between the highest and lowest volume levels in any audio program. A compressor is a device that squeezes that dynamic range. The compression ratio is the ratio of output level change to input level change measured in dB. In a conventional compressor/limiter, normal program dynamics are heard until the input level rises above a preset threshold. At this point, the gain suddenly begins to be reduced by a fixed ratio. One of the applications is to smooth out variations in microphone level. When the distance between a vocalist and a microphone changes, variations in signal level occur. If the compressor is adjusted for low compression (around 2:1), these variations can be smoothed. The same can be done for musical instruments. Compression lessens the loudness variations among the strings and increases the sustain. Other instruments, such as horns, vary in loudness depending on the note being played, and benefit similarly.

With programs of widely varying levels, compression can prevent recording levels from saturating tape tracks. Compressors are frequently used to prevent excessive program levels from damaging drivers in sound-reinforcement systems. A limiter is a compressor with a high compression ration, usually 10:1 or higher. A limiter begins its operatin only above a certain input level called the threshold. Limiting also benefits intelligibility by allowing low-level input signals to be reproduced through the system at higher volume. In a musical performance, this provides additional intimacy as the vocalist's whispers are heard clearly at each seat in the house.

As a general rule, the compressors should be as close to the amplifiers as possible in the signal chain. If the compressor is placed before the EQ, for example, a potentially damaging boost in EQ won't be seen by the compressor and the speakers may be damaged.

The compressor works by providing a gradual increase in the ratio of gain reduction as the input signal approaches and exceeds the preset threshold. Either peak detection or the more desirable rms detection can be used in compressors. For example, the dbx 903 acts as an rms-based absolute limiter at a compression ratio setting of infinity:1, and holds program material at or below a fixed output level. At settings beyond infinity:1, the 903 actually reduces the output signal whenever the input level exceeds the threshold setting. With infinity+ compression an apparent dynamic inversion can be achieved, making the 903 capable of producing unusual special effects with percussive signal envelopes. Threshold sensitivity usually falls between -40 dB and +20 dB. The compression ratio can also be adjusted from 1:1 (no compression) through increasing ratios until infinite compression. The output gain is controllable from -20 dB to +20 dB, allowing the output level to be increased or decreased as necessary.

Range Expanders

A range expander increases the signal fed into its input by a given ratio. An expansion ratio of 2:1 means that for a 1 dB change of level at the input, a 2 dB change of level appears at the output of the expander. An expander can restore some of the dynamic range lost in a compressor earlier in the signal path. It is important that expansion does not begin below the noise level of the system. Expansion, limiting and gate functions are sometimes combined on one instrument.

Aural Exciters

Quite a few years ago a man named Curt Knoppel was building a stereo tube amplifier. Once completed, he found one channel to be working perfectly while the other sounded strange. For no apparent reason, he connected the "bad" channel to the "good" one and found that it enhanced the original signal. The Aural Exciter was born.

The first model introduced to the public also used tubes, and it was not sold, but rented by the minute. Back in those days, recordings were made in acoustically dead studios where everything was closed-miked. Mixdowns were made to quarter-inch tape, at 15 IPS and usually with noise reduction. Aural excitement, added at the disc-mastering stage, brought life to mixes that seemed dull and/or lacking ambience.

Basically, the process is a combination of phase and amplitude distortion that, when added to a track or mix, does what EQ alone cannot do. An Aural Exciter is a psychoacoustic processor that increases brilliance not by equalization, but by adding harmonics not present in the original sound. Inside, a variable high-pass filter is used to roll off all frequencies below 1 kHz. In the process of filtering, a certain amount of phase shift and harmonic distortion occurs. After the filter, the signal is sent to a limiter that distorts in a musical way and makes the signal peaks seem louder. This is now called a harmonics generator because it generates musically related harmonics. The processed signal is now mixed back with the original, creating an enhanced effect that tickles your ear in a psychoacoustic way. The signal seems louder, but it is not. Because a high-pass filter is used, the sound is brighter across a wide frequency spectrum.

The result is a perceived increase in mid- and high-frequency response. This is not the same as boosting certain parts of the frequency spectrum with EQ, nor is it similar to inserting a high-pass filter in line. You do not hear evident boosts at certain frequencies. Aural excitement increases intelligibility, enhances stereo imaging, and creates increased presence and clarity.

Practical uses for an aural exciter are easy to find. In the studio, it can be used at any stage from tracking to mixdown, or afterward to improve the sound of cassette copies. In a live situation, the exciter could be used to add an extra presence to a poor guitar sound, or just to improve the overall sound of the entire mix. It could also save high-frequency drivers from being destroyed. It is recommended for anyone looking for the extra "zing" in their sound.

Warning: The exciter will also enhance certain high-end recording noise such as tape hiss. It does its job no matter what the program material might be. One suggestion is to use noise reduction in the signal path to defeat the potential problem.

Noise Gates

The basic purpose of a noise gate is to remove unwanted background sounds in the spaces between desired foreground sounds. Note that there has to be some real level distance between the unwanted and wanted material—at least a few dB—in order for the noise gate to "get its foot in the door." If levels are too much the same (because of compression, for example), the downward-expansion efforts of the unit will go for naught. Therefore, use noise gates *before* any compressors.

A noise gate may be used to prevent or reduce leakage among microphones in live-sound reinforcement and during panel discussions. Placing a unit on each mike and setting its threshold below the level of the music or speech will achieve this. It can also be used during a remote interview to attenuate the noise from wind or air conditioning.

There are many possibilities for noise gates in a recording studio or on stage. Sound engineers can clean up a buzzy drum kit, or keep a closely miked piano track from being "contaminated" by leakage from a second instrument (e.g., a drum). This potential leakage applies to each drum in the kit. By gating out such leakage, a noise gate on each microphone will help it pick up only direct sound. The result is a tight, close-up sound from each individual drum.

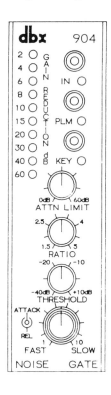

Figure 33. dbx 904 Noise Gate

A noise gate, like the dbx 904, is a very fast, voltage-controlled, below-threshold downward expander. It senses the level of an input or a keying signal and determines whether this level is below the front-panel threshold setting. If so, the signal gets attenuated; if not, it passes at unity (0 dB) gain. The amount that the signal is attenuated is a function both of its own level and of the settings of the attenuation, limit, ratio and threshold knobs.

As with other dynamic-range manipulators, nothing educates the user like thorough experimentation. "Hands-on" familiarity with this device will prove irreplaceable.

Parametric Equalization

The electronic device having the most flexibility in adjusting the tones and frequency response of a signal is the

12. Signal Processing and Effects

parametric equalizer. All of the "parameters" of equalization are controlled: the frequencies you want to modify, the amount of cut or boost, and the bandwidth of the frequency you are filtering. Using a parametric equalizer, you can select the range of frequencies you want to adjust, then define the narrow band of sound that you really want without disturbing any adjacent frequencies. Parametric equalization is especially helpful in vocal reinforcement or in feedback situations. The gremlin frequencies can be isolated and cut to establish a consistent response pattern with maximum headroom.

The dbx 905 is a typical parametric equalizer. It has three center-frequency adjustable filters. The high end extends from 800 to 20,000 Hz, the mid from 200 to 5000 Hz, and the low from 20 to 500 Hz. The amount of gain or attenuation at the filter's center frequency is then adjusted using a rotary potentiometer. There are LEDs to indicate clipping at any key circuit point.

Graphic Equalization

Graphic equalizers normally incorporate sliding potentiometers giving about a 12 dB boost or cut when required. A typical graphic equalizer will provide two full channels of 1/3 octave equalization in one unit. The Klark-Teknik DN-360 has thirty 1/3 octave ISO standard frequencies per channel. To understand the concept of 1/3 octave, just remember the following principles. If a frequency is doubled or halved, that represents one octave. For instance, 440 Hz is the "A" used to tune on a piano. Therefore, 220 Hz is the first "A" below and 880 Hz is the first "A" above. Divide these octaves into thirds and you will realize what frequencies you are adjusting with a 1/3 octave graphic equalizer. One thing to remember with regard to graphic equalizers: when you are adjusting one potentiometer and attempting to cut or boost a range (1/3 octave) of frequencies, you are also adjusting the adjacent frequencies as well. Some graphic equalizers are better than others, but none will allow you to isolate frequencies the way parametric equalizers will.

Digital Effects Generators

A digital effects generator uses highly refined LSI (large scale integration) technology to create natural reverberation. It is an electronic device that may have several effects stored in memory (ROM, or read-only memory that can't be changed by the user) as well as the capability of designing your own effects and storing those in memory. This is accomplished by selecting a preset effect and adjusting the parameters to suit your requirements.

The Yamaha SPX-90 is a moderately priced digital multi-effect processor that contains 30 preset effects comprehensive enough to suit most studio and performance applications. It also allows the user to create up to 60 additional effects and store them for instant recall. The SPX-90 can create effects far beyond reverberation. A variety of echo, delay, and special effects, each with comprehensive parameter adjustments, can

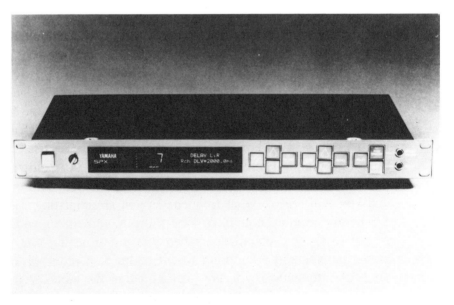

Figure 34. Yamaha SPX–90 Digital Effects Processor

12. Signal Processing and Effects

be accessed at the touch of a switch. As the SPX-90 is MIDI-compatible, it can be programmed to apply separate effects to a number of MIDI-compatible instruments. It is useful in a variety of situations: acoustic, electric, PA, MIDI instrument and home recording systems. To ensure that user programs are not lost when the power is turned off, a built-in long-life battery acts as a backup. In normal use, the battery will last five years, but it is advisable to change the battery before this time has elapsed.

Sound Effects

There is a wide variety of sound effects available on record, tape and compact disc. The BBC sound effects library is a good place to start. There are also CD sound effect collections available. These are very clean, often recorded digitally as well as mastered. See the Product Resource Directory in Appendix C for the names and addresses of these sources.

You can always make your own sound effects. In Lily Tomlin's one woman Broadway show, *The Search for Intelligent Life in the Universe*, she worked extensively with her sound designer to come up with concrete sound effects: chains for the punk teenager, a hot-water bottle sloshing for a waterbed sound. The most effective means of creating customized sound effects is by working together with the artist to create the ideal sound for the dramatic context.

13. MIDI, Sampling and Computers

The MIDI Interface

As keyboardists struggled with the headaches of integrating growing stacks of instruments into a single controllable system, some instrument designers recognized the need for a control signal interface standard for digitally-based musical instruments which would enable a musician to control one or more instruments from a master controller. A standard was formally proposed by Sequential in 1981. By the summer of 1982 several manufacturers had agreed on a modified form of the proposal, and the musical instrument digital interface (MIDI) was born. Instruments from two different manufacturers were first MIDI-ed together in January 1983. Since then, the MIDI scene has been growing explosively, and with few serious glitches. This has spawned the development of specialized performance controllers and sequencers. It also encourages the use of computers with synthesizers. Musicians have access to a multitude of new software packages for composing, score-writing, and sound synthesis.

MIDI is essentially a communication language that enables various digital devices to communicate with each other. MIDI allows devices to communicate by converting their actions into a language that can be transmitted by wires connecting the devices. The MIDI language, as with almost all other digital devices, uses the binary system as its codes for communicating. These binary codes (called bits) are transmitted at a very high rate of about 31,250 ($\pm$ 1%) bits per second (baud). Because the data is transmitted at such a fast rate, it permits musical devices to communicate in real time, allowing practically instant communication and response between the devices. The hardware and software standard was initially created for live performances but has been used extensively in studio and composition environments.

Each MIDI-equipped instrument usually contains a receiver and a transmitter. Some instruments may have only one or the other. The receiver receives messages in MIDI format and executes MIDI commands. It consists of an optoisolator, Universal Asynchronous Receiver/Transmitter (UART), and other hardware needed to perform the intended

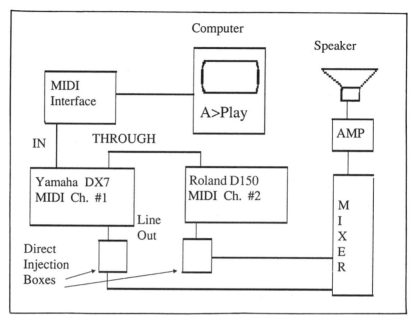

Figure 35. MIDI hookup

functions. The transmitter originates messages in MIDI format and transmits them by way of a UART and line driver. The interface operates asynchronously, with a start bit, 8 data bits (D0 to D7), and a stop bit. This makes a total of 10 bits for a period of 320 microseconds per serial byte.

The MIDI data generated by one instrument is sent to others as serial data over a single line. In serial data transmission, the bits are sent one after the other rather than simultaneously (requiring more wires). The bits are then received and collected in groups to be converted to a message or command by the receiving devices.

The MIDI codes or bits are not the actual sounds created by the instrument in digital form. They are a representation of the mechanics of how the sound was created. The actual sounds produced by the instrument are provided at the "line out" terminal and are completely independent of the MIDI network. MIDI codes do not recognize or care what the sound was that created them, MIDI cannot attempt to classify sounds since an infinite number of sounds exist. MIDI codes allow musical devices to respond to the actions of other devices and be driven by their commands. For example, if two keyboards are connected by a MIDI line, one of the keyboards can drive the other and make it create sounds without actually touching the second keyboard. The sound created by the second keyboard is not dependent on the sound produced by the first keyboard, but reveals what the first keyboard would sound like if it had the second built into it.

In MIDI, details such as whether the key, or note, is turned on or off, or the position of the levers and switches and the patch/program settings, are sent over a wire in digital form.

MIDI commands are composed of three bytes of eight bits. Each byte has its own purpose. The first byte of a MIDI command is called the status byte. It contains information such as "note on" or "note off," channel numbers, real-time controller changes, program changes and more. Each of the different commands has its own unique arrangements of 0s and 1s. The second byte is a data byte and contains information such as the key number if the status byte is a "note on" byte. The third byte is also a data byte with more detailed information relating to the status byte.

MIDI connections are made by attaching the MIDI devices through MIDI lines which consist of five wires with 5-pin DIN connectors on the ends. See Figure 35 for a typical MIDI configuration.

Sequencers

A sequencer is a word processor for music. It is a computer-based device that accepts as input the data transmitted by any MIDI keyboard or other controller. Once inside the machine, the data can be altered, played back, or stored in permanent form. Computers can create MIDI data from software packages and play that data on any number of digital instruments. This allows entire compositions to be created and performed from a computer keypad without ever touching a synthesizer or instrument. Cakewalk is a software program for the IBM from Twelve Tone Systems that turns the computer into a sequencer. Columns display track, channel, event time in bar/beat/clock format, event type, and up to three data fields associated with the event type. These fields may contain information as to pitch (octave number), velocity and duration. Channel information includes such things as note-on and note-off, pitch bends and after-touch. System information includes start, stop, continue, timing clocks, and song position pointers. The computer is connected to a MIDI-equipped keyboard or other instrument. Interface hardware is needed to send MIDI signals through the computer. The MIDI specification requires a current loop serial interface. There are MIDI interfaces available for most popular computers. The Atari ST has built-in MIDI ports.

One example of MIDI in action was the 1987 tour by the rock group Chicago. The tour, dubbed the "MIDI tour," was appropriately named. The band used small devices that converted analog signals to MIDI data. These were linked to a large computer/MIDI network behind the stage. Every instrument on stage, except for the vocal mics, was connected to this computer network. At the center of this system were two computer operators who sat in front of computer terminals "directing traffic." Massive sampling data storage systems and memory units were connected to the computer system. The result of all of this was that the audience almost never heard the actual instruments. Instead they heard samples of studio recorded instruments stored in the network. The computer operators were able to completely change the sound of every instrument after each song.

Lighting manufacturers are beginning to incorporate MIDI benefits into their systems. With MIDI, lighting chase rates can be synchronized to a clock. Cues may be programmed into the lighting console and then the console can be treated as a MIDI channel device. A MIDI-event will trigger light cues just as it may initiate an audible event. Consoles with MIDI compatibility are available now. Among the leaders in this technology are Sun, NSI, Leprecon/CAE and ETC. As a memory tool, MIDI is incredible, but it hasn't been used in full-blown touring applications for lighting yet. Perhaps this is because MIDI consoles are limited to 32 channels currently. Many software designers for lighting control consoles are becoming familiar with MIDI and we should see more innovative products before too long.

Synthesis

Robert Moog's name has been a household word among musicians since his groundbreaking work with voltage-controlled synthesizers in the 1960s. By 1975, the synthesizer scene, such as it was, was dominated by ARP instruments and Moog Music. Roland and Korg were just getting started while Oberheim was sliding into the packaged synthesizer market with its expander modules. In an article for the first issue of *Contemporary Keyboard*, Robert Moog defined what a synthesizer is. At the time, most people, even most keyboardists, didn't know. The answers, which were developed in succeeding issues, had to do with oscillators, filters, and amplifiers. There was no worry about microprocessors or channel assignment modes. In those days it was taken for granted that an electronic keyboardist should be able to follow a patching diagram or a computer program flow chart. But in 1975, performing keyboardists were just starting to feel comfortable with simple synthesizer controls. However, the history of synthesizers owes as much to the vagaries of business as it does to technological breakthroughs or inventive geniuses. Without a doubt, the foremost of these breakthroughs is the proliferation of the microprocessor.

A microprocessor is a digital integrated circuit that contains all the computation and program execution circuits needed to implement a small computer or digital controller.

Equipped with the right object code (i.e., operating programs), a microprocessor is capable of performing many sophisticated tasks inside an electronic musical instrument: keyboard scanning, parameter assignment, envelope and modulation waveform generation, automatic oscillator tuning, and so on.

In the early 1970s, Keith Emerson used a ribbon controller for both musical expression and theatrical gesture. Now musicians have touch-sensitive keys that are designed to allow

Figure 36. Yamaha DX7IIFD Digital Synthesizer (Courtesy Yamaha   Corporation)

the player to shape tones naturally. Key pressure can vary loudness, brightness, or pitch. Keyboardists are aware of the musical importance of responsive keyboards.

13. MIDI, Sampling and Computers

Sampling

According to legend, the Fairlight was originally conceived in the mid–'70s as a harmonic and waveform synthesis system. Sound sampling was added, almost as an afterthought, when the designers discovered that their synthesis design included 95% of the hardware needed to sample sounds from the outside world. The Fairlight's success appears to be due primarily to its sound sampling capability, which allows the user to musically manipulate any sound that can be recorded. Shortly thereafter, E-mu introduced the Emulater and Ray Kurzweil developed the Kurzweil 250 which included sounds in permanent memory ROM. Ensoniq's Mirage made basic sampling capabilities available at a bargain price.

In Chapter 1 we discussed the nature of sound waves and the regular pattern of peaks and troughs called frequencies. A single peak and trough pair is called a cycle, and sound is most often discussed in terms of the number of cycles per second, or Hertz (Hz). If a sound has 30 or 40 cycles per second, it is said to have a low frequency or pitch, and if 10,000 cycles are happening per second, it has a very high frequency. It is important to understand that sounds in the real world are not made up of simple, mathematically pure waves. A human being can listen to a woodwind quintet holding a sustained chord and tell without much difficulty which note is being played by the flute, which by the oboe, and which by the French horn. This type of analysis is still beyond the power of any computer program yet written.

When a sound is converted into fluctuations in electrical voltage using a microphone, the voltage fluctuations are smooth and continuous. The voltage is an analog of the air pressure: higher pressure, higher voltage. If the microphone is a good one, the voltage waves will resemble very closely the sound waves that gave rise to them. If the microphone is not a good one, distortion of the waves will occur.

Now comes the tricky part. When we've got an analog voltage that is fluctuating in a smooth, continuous manner, between 0 volts and +10 volts, let's say, it can have literally an infinite number of values, 3.1415926535 volts for example. The computer likes to see this number as a digital value, so we decide what increments the computer can handle. For example, if we are dealing with analog signals between 0 and 10 volts, we might decide to divide this range up into .01-volt increments. Each step (.03, 1.76, 8.20 volts, etc.,) would be assigned its own number for computer purposes. Now the computer is in an ideal position to take a "snapshot" of the voltage as it exists at a given moment in time and assign that voltage value to a computer number. The device that performs this operation is called an analog-to-digital (A/D) converter, and it is the heart of the digital sampling process.

One snapshot won't do much good because the voltage is constantly fluctuating. A short time later we need to take another snapshot, then another. In order to get any kind of a meaningful picture of the waveform, we need to take a lot of snapshots, or samples, and we need to take them very quickly. The speed with which we take samples is called the sampling rate. The basic rule is that the sampling rate must be at least twice as fast as the highest frequency to be sampled. If we want to sample sounds at 20 kHz, the sampling rate must be at least 40 kHz. That is 40,000 samples every second. Pro audio sampling rates tend to be slightly higher than this: 41.9 kHz, 44.1 kHz, or even 50 kHz. The Nyquist frequency is half the sampling rate. It refers to the highest frequency that a given device can safely sample.

Numbers are stored in digital memories as groups of binary (two-state) digits, called bits. Each bit in a sample accounts for a factor of two in the accuracy of a digital number. Thus, if a sample is recorded as an 8-bit number, that means the dynamic range of the input waveform is divided into 256 (two raised to the eighth power) possible levels, and one of those levels is recorded. Of course, audio waveforms vary continuously, so the process of dividing the sampled waveform in 256 levels introduces error. This error is heard as noise or as distortion. If you follow the math through, you see that each additional bit per sample reduces the error by 6 dB. For an 8-bit sample, the error is 48 dB below the maximum signal. Early real-sound instruments used 8-bit sampling. Now most of the line instruments use 16 bits.

Computers

Sound control has been advanced with the utilization of computers. Futuristic special effects, once relegated to science fiction, are now commonplace. From simple programmable delays to effects processing and digital control, microprocessors are used for an increasing number of functions. The dawn of the digital audio workstation with a control computer as its brain is here with products made by Soundstream, JVC, 3M, Sony and CompuSonics. The new tools of the industry, as important as loudspeakers and microphones, will be digital gain controls, automatic mixers, equalizers, switching matrices, monitors and testing devices.

A computer interface for sound installations has been proposed using an RS-422 serial interface which would set an industry standard for digital control protocol. This type of interface allows control over great distances. The effective limit of the RS-232 standard, familiar to computer users already, is approximately 50 feet, whereas the RS-422 can be run nearly a mile. The interface will be capable of linking different types of computers and microprocessors, and the receiving equipment will let the sending unit know it has received the data.

The special nature of theatre requires a variety of sources and locations for sound reproduction. The computer is ideal for flexibility of speaker selection, multiple inputs and remote control. Altec has developed a program called Acousta-CADD, which analyzes the elements of sound in an environment. Imagine interfacing this with other devices. Knowing all of the parameters of the sound system and room, the computer could adjust all of the appropriate levels of microphones and speakers as well as set delays and equalization for any microphone position chosen.

Some of the new products are unique and exciting. Oxmoor Corporation has a remote digital volume control system and digital control equalizer. An external Macintosh computer is used with trademark TWEEQ software for display of mouse-driven graphics. The software allows fast flipping between stored curves for A-B comparisons. T.C. Electronic of Denmark has introduced a combination graphic equalizer and spectrum analyzer capable of tracking feedback on a "search and destroy" basis.

Somewhere software designers are hard at work developing a library of "icons," representational pictures that graphically portray functions such as "increase loudness," or "stop tape," or "cut speaker #4." It is conceivable that before long an operator will be able to select a location, such as stage left proscenium, on the display CRT with a light pen or mouse. Once the microphone is plugged into the selected location, the operator might use the computer to control and fine tune the microphone and loudspeaker characteristics to suit the venue.

Richmond Sound in Vancouver has developed the Command/Cue matrix which uses an Amiga computer with programmable crosspoint switches to control up to an astonishing 4,096 faders. This massive task is accomplished smoothly, quickly and effortlessly. It can execute an almost limitless number of cues of enormous complexity, including fades, loops, clock-timed follows, effects and pans. The computer is a 68000 processor based with a proprietary 32-bit parallel interface. It runs previously stored cue sequences, and may be used as a sequencer to send and receive MIDI messages.

Yet, despite the complexity of its operation, the Command/Cue system is designed for intuitive use. Live and programmed digital audio control is possible. It has a graphic

13. MIDI, Sampling and Computers

representation of a virtual panel so that a large number of inputs and outputs may be controlled. Screens are arranged functionally, and alphanumeric descriptions may be assigned to individual cues.

The computer can electronically patch loudspeaker and amplifier configuration. When speaker lines are installed in new facilities, it is advisable to run a separate line for each receptacle location, rather than parallel multiple outlets. This will allow future accommodation of computer-selected output routing. The possibilities are limitless.

A new chip from Motorola called a digital signal processing chip (DSP) is one of the fastest available for processing complex audio signals. It is used in the new computer from Next, Inc. and sets a standard for future microcomputer design. It is ideal for analyzing or manipulating sounds. For instance, a soprano could have her voice recorded in digital form via a microphone attached to the computer. The DSP chip will store her voice in digital form. Then it could play it back with CD quality or alter the voice in some other way. When the Next computer debuted, it accompanied a live cellist with a synthesized harpsichord.

This chapter is still being written. Computers are being used now to control the movement of sound on stage by automatic panning and output selection. They are also being used as sequencers to control the output of multiple MIDI devices. Many mixing consoles contain microprocessor circuitry, small computers for automatic gain and EQ control. The digital amplifier is described in Chapter 4 of this book. Nearly every electronic device has the potential of benefitting from computer technology. The Sound Designer should be content with nothing less than a system that allows the creation of sound as a transparent extension of the imagination and desire of the artist.

14. Acoustics

Description

In the broadest sense, acoustics is the science dealing with sound. Chapter 1 considered many fundamental elements of acoustics such as frequency, response to tones and intensity. Subsequent chapters dealt with different methods of propagating, recording and transmitting sound and how to route and control the output. In this chapter, acoustics will be considered in a more restrictive sense. It is concerned with those qualities of a space that have to do with how clearly sounds can be heard in it. The focus is on the interaction between the environment and the source and how it affects production, transmission and perception of music or speech. In an enclosed space, reflection, absorption and diffusion of walls, ceiling, floor or any solid objects may contribute as much or more to the sound than the direct path from source to listener.

Sound is created by materials that vibrate. Molecules of air are set in motion, producing an outward traveling wave. It may move for a few hundred or several thousand feet. Sound travels at 1130 feet per second in air. Sound travels much faster under water and increases as the water gets deeper. Divers filming underwater volcanoes on the south shore of Hawaii, the "big island," encountered deafening sounds from the flowing rock that sent shock waves strong enough to move their masks. Of course, in the theatre, air is the primary transmission medium. However, today's audience does not sit on a hillside as in the sunny outdoor theatre of ancient Greece. Instead, carpet, glass, wood, gypsum board, airconditioning, street noise and concrete surround the spectator and affect the sound waves that color the listener's perception.

The study of acoustic properties provides a means for analyzing how the initial vibration, whether it be from a loudspeaker cone, violin string or actor's vocal chord, travels through air, encounters interfering surfaces, is reflected or absorbed and finally reaches the listener's ear.

Sound for the Stage

For an understanding of acoustics and definition of terms, it is necessary to turn to several important sources. The single best source for acoustics remains *Music, Acoustics and Architecture* by Leo Beranek. He completed a 6-year study of 54 concert halls in 1962. The book presents physical data on the halls, along with the expressed preferences of many professional musicians, including conductors, performers and music critics. From this material he extrapolated those acoustical qualities that contributed most to the success of a hall and evaluated in numerical terms their relative importance. This research provided a way to evaluate acoustics. Another useful source is Dr. George C. Izenour's *Theatre Design* which is to theatre architecture what Beranek's book is to concert hall acoustics. Rollins Brook has contributed to the knowledge of acoustics and updated many fundamental concepts in a chapter titled "Rooms for Speech, Music and Cinema," found in the *Handbook for Sound Engineers*. All of these sources should be consulted for a complete understanding of acoustics.

Myths

One of the persistent myths of acoustics is that there are no definite rules. However, the theoretical foundations of acoustics were established late in the nineteenth century by the English physicist Lord Raleigh. Wallace C. Sabine, a 27-year-old assistant professor, was approached in 1895 by President Eliot of Harvard to improve the acoustics of the Fogg Art Museum in Cambridge. His colleagues warned him that the problem was so complex that a complete solution was hopeless. After five years of research he gave to acoustics the classical reverberation equation and made the first advances in the application of acoustics to architecture. Before electronic equipment was invented, it was not possible to verify the data that Sabine produced. Once the amplifier, loudspeaker and microphone were available, acousticians were able to produce and accurately measure sounds consistent with Sabine's theory. Without these tools, previous designers of theatres and performing halls could only learn about acoustics by listening to past successes and failures, and speculating as to what was responsible for each. It is no wonder that the study of acoustics is surrounded with an air of mystery.

Among the arcane beliefs are that paint on the wall, gold leaf on the statues, wooden beams in the wings, or broken wine bottles under the stage will benefit the sound of a hall. As mentioned in the Introduction, the Greek theatre had excellent acoustics. But when the manager of a world-famous concert hall said that his hall had perfect acoustics because one could hear the sound of a pin dropped on the stage from anywhere in it, Eugene Ormandy replied, "I don't want to hear a pin drop, I want to hear the orchestra." Acoustics are not merely concerned with projection of faint sounds from the stage to the most distant seats.

Some other beliefs are that small halls generally sound better than large ones, that halls built to serve many purposes are inferior to ones built especially for concert or opera, that a wooden interior is required for good acoustics and that old halls sound better than new ones. It has been proven repeatedly that excellent acoustics can be heard in a large hall. It is also a misconception that steel, glass and concrete cannot be used effectively. In order to keep the sound energy inside of a concert hall the walls are usually made hard and heavy. Of course, it may be necessary to add other absorptive materials in combination with reverberant ones to modify an environment to become acoustically effective for a variety of production modes. As to whether acoustics improve as the hall ages, that may have more to do with the reputation of a particular hall or the growing acceptance of regular patrons over a period of time.

Attributes

Following is a description of attributes originally suggested by Beranek in his investigation of musical and acoustical qualities:

Sound for the Stage

Intimacy: Indicates to a listener the size of the room. It is not necessary that it actually be a particular size, but only that it sound as though it is. An intimate hall has presence. The listener's impression of the size of a hall is determined by the the interval between the sound that arrives directly at his ear and the first reflection that arrives there from the walls or ceiling. This interval is also called the initial-time-delay gap. In Beranek's study, intimacy was considered to be three times as important as any other attribute.

Liveness: A hall that is reverberant is called a live hall. A room that reflects too little is dead or dry. A live room is often said to be acoustically superior to a dead room. In most halls, seats that have poor sight lines also have defective acoustics. Room size has a lot to do with liveness. If the cubic volume is large for the size of the audience and the interior surfaces are sound reflective, it will be live.

Warmth: A hall may be live, but deficient in bass. Fullness of bass tone relative to the mid-frequency tone gives the impression of warmth. To state this another way, a hall will have a warm sound if frequencies below 250 Hz have longer reverb times than the frequencies between 500 and 1000 Hz. A full, rich bass gives a warm sound. Too much bass is called boomy. If the lows have a shorter reverberation time, the sound is said to be brittle.

Loudness of direct sound: In a small hall the direct sound will reach the back rows with adequate loudness. If the hall is too large, the effect of the inverse square law is felt. Intensity will decrease in direct proportion to the square of the distance. Loudness will then be too low by the time it reaches the distant listeners. Direct sound is usually at its best about 60 feet from the stage.

Loudness of reverberant sound: This is related to the intensity of sound that does not travel directly to the listener and the to reberberation time of the hall. It is inversely related to the cubic volume of a hall and upon total absorption.

14. Acoustics

Definition or clarity: A hall has definition when the sound is clear and distinct. A hall that lacks definition is described as blurry or muddy. This attribute is related to intimacy, liveness and loudness of direct and reverberant sound. It is a combination of four of the previous five attributes.

Brilliance: A bright, clear, ringing sound rich in harmonics is described as brilliant. It is affected by the initial-time-delay gap. A hall that has liveness, clarity and intimacy has brilliant sound.

Diffusion: This attribute concerns the orientation of the reverberant sound in space. It is best when the reverberant sound arrives at the listener's ear from all directions in equal amounts. Irregular interior surfaces and long reverberation times will diffuse the sound. Diffusion will be lacking if a hall has smooth side walls and ceiling which discourage cross reflections and scattering of the sound waves. Poor diffusion may result also when the stage area is reverberant but the rest of the hall is dead.

Other attributes are balance, blend, ensemble, texture, freedom from echo, freedom from noise, dynamic range, tonal quality and uniformity. Since these last nine attributes primarily apply to musical performance and not theatre, detailed descriptions are omitted.

Room Size

The enormous stone cathedrals of the middle ages, with lengthy reverberation times, were well suited for hymns and religious ceremonies. Since the Mass was celebrated in Latin and understood by few outside of the clergy, intelligibility was not an issue. The entire space, audience and stage of Shakespeare's Globe would have fit within the orchestra of Epidaurus. The relatively short distance between actor and audience and the importance of the spoken word made the Elizabethan theatre an ideal space for dramatic performance. The Guthrie Theatre in Minneapolis is overall only slightly wider than the Greek *skene*. Max Reinhardt's Grosses Schauspielhaus was three times the size of the Guthrie, but not even half of Epidaurus.

Throughout history, composers have written with a particular space in mind. A perfect example is the music-drama of Richard Wagner written for the Festspielhaus in Bayreuth. The Redoutensaal in Vienna existed in Beethoven's time. It seated about 400 people and had a reverberation time with full audience of about 1.4 seconds at mid frequencies. Many of the larger halls of the nineteenth century had reverberation times of over 2 seconds. Music sounds louder in a hall that has long reverberation times, particularly in the rear of the hall. It enhances the bass.

The university campus facility is often designed for multiple use including lecture, drama, dance, orchestra, musical comedy and cinema. Since music has a greater dynamic range and a greater frequency range than speech, the first step in designing a multi-purpose hall is to decide what the priority of the facility will be. Is it a concert hall, a road house, or a drama playhouse? If the choice is for the spoken word, then each time music is performed the reverberation time must be raised somehow. If the hall is designed for music, something must be done to lower the reverberation time for speech, which may then require a reinforcement system for sufficient volume and clarity. Since the impact of a concert or musical comedy often depends upon the loudness that the performing group can achieve, it is crucial to know that loudness varies with room volume and with audience size. These factors must be taken into account when designing the performance space.

Initial-time-delay gap

A listener's impression of the size of the hall is determined by the initial-time-delay gap (ITDG), the interval between the sound that arrives directly at his ear and the first reflection that arrives there from the walls or ceiling. Figure 37 shows a graphic representation of the difference between the arrival of

14. Acoustics

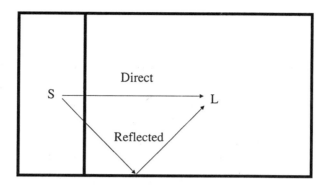

Figure 37. ITDG for a rectangular room

the direct sound and the arrival of the first reflection in a simple rectangular room. It is clear from this analysis that as the width and height of the hall change, so will the initial-time-delay gap.

The principle problem associated with a hall of large cubic volume is a too long initial-time-delay gap at the ears of many of the listeners. If the ITDG is as short as 19 milliseconds, the acoustics may be excellent. An ITDG greater than 49 milliseconds suggests an acoustic property that is less than adequate. Research has determined that the ITDG should be less than 25 milliseconds, or 25 one-thousandths of a second, for clarity and intelligibility.

Corrective measures may consist of sound-reflecting surfaces hung horizontally between the ceiling and the main floor. Panels have been employed either to shorten the initial-time-delay gap, to prevent the unfortunate focusing of sounds from curved ceilings or to direct the upper registers of the strings over the heads of the front of an audience seated on a flat floor to the listeners at the back. Reflecting panels were used as early as 1953 by Lothar Cremer in reconstructing the Herkelessaal in Munich. Bolt, Beranek and Newman, Inc.

used similar panels in Caracas, Venezuela in 1954, and in the Kresge Auditorium in Cambridge, Massachusetts in 1955.

At the University of California at Berkeley in the early 1970s, an acoustic consultant was asked to retune Zellerbach Hall. A Real-Time Analyzer was used to determine which surfaces needed treatment. Then plaster was added or subtracted to create an ideal reflection/absorption pattern. The result was a subtle yet effective change that revealed the violins in the orchestra much better than before. Today's designers and consultants are adept at using moveable panels to change the acoustics of a hall to suit the particular performance whether it be drama, opera or symphony. Often these panels are electronically controlled. New concert halls, such as the Performing Arts Center in Tampa, may have a combination of moveable panels, curtains and walls that can be altered for a specific type of performance.

The current era is characterized by the implementation of variable acoustic systems and electronics has replaced architecture as the controller of acoustics in some multipurpose auditoriums. Decoustics, a Canadian manufacturer of acoustic products, is one manufacturer of a system that electronically changes the acoustics of a space to suit different kinds of productions. Called the Acoustical Control System (ACS), it consists of an array of microphones and speakers controlled by a central processor. The sound as heard by the microphones is analyzed and the speaker output is modified to correct problems created by reverberation and absorption.

Reverberance

Reverberance is generally defined as the time required for the sound pressure level in an enclosed space to decrease 60 dB.

14. Acoustics

Reverberation depends upon:

1. the length of the reverberation time

2. the loudness of sound relative to background noise

3. the ratio of the loudness of the reverberant to the direct sound.

The direction of reverberation is also important, since early reflections off of side walls are now recognized as having a greater effect on intimacy than those from above or behind the audience. Later reflections should be perceived as arriving simultaneously from all directions. Reverberance is a major factor in liveness, loudness and clarity. Too little reverberance will degrade the first two attributes, too much will degrade the last.

Rooms designed for speech work best with a reverberation time less than 1.5 seconds, preferably under a second. Halls designed for music will have good acoustics if the reverberation time is slightly more than 1.5 seconds. A performance of Bach organ music or choral recitals will benefit from longer reverberation times. Lectures and drama will have better articulation with shorter reverberation times. Opera and musical comedy falls somewhere in between these two extremes.

Intelligibility

Clarity is the degree to which individual sounds stand apart. It is related to reverberation and background noise, including sounds both inside and outside of the hall. Therefore, heat, ventilation and air conditioning will affect intelligibility as will traffic or machinery operated in the near vicinity.

The requirements for the hearing of speech and conditions that must be realized in the design of a multiple use auditorium are listed in the chapter of Izenour's book written by Vern Knudsen titled "Acoustical Design of Multiple-Use Auditoria." These criteria, which are abbreviated and summarized here, are also mentioned and further defined by Rol-

Sound for the Stage

lins Brook in the *Handbook for Sound Engineers*. The guidelines are:

1. The speaker must speak loudly enough or his speech must be amplified

2. The room must be free from noise and excessive reverberation

3. The shape of the room must be designed so that it is free from echoes and interfering reflections in order to provide the optimal distribution of reflected sound to all listeners

4. If the speech is not amplified, as is usual in a small auditorium or an intimate theatre, the speaker must face the audience or face nearby reflective surfaces that reflect speech energy to the audience.

Rooms must not be:

1. Afflicted with interfering or masking noises like heat, ventilation and air-conditioning equipment (HVAC)

2. Impaired with echoes or other interfering reflections

3. Disturbed by focusing effects like concave surfaces

4. So diffuse that it prevents localization and identification of the sources of sound on the stage.

Rooms should be contructed with:

1. Optimal dimensions and shape for the generation and distribution of sustained and impulsive sounds of early and delayed reflections from all wall and ceiling surfaces

2. Growth and decay characteristics at all frequencies that are adjustable between live and dead for speech and music

3. Diffusion of reflected sound for low-, mid- and high-frequencies so that direct sound heard by the audience will be enhanced by successive reflections of the sound which will flow smoothly to the listener from all directions. This gives the audience the feeling that they are immersed in sound.

Absorption

Absorbing materials are used in acoustics to control unwanted reflections and to reduce overall reverberation time of the room. Absorption may be used to tune a room for speech or music. For good speech reinforcement the reverberation time should be uniform from 200 to 4000 Hz, although a small increase in reverberation time around 500 Hz is acceptable. Large rooms will show the effect of air absorption above 2000 Hz. There are three types of absorption:

Absorption Coefficients of Selected Materials
(sabins per square foot)

material	frequency 125	250	500	1 k	2k	4k
Brick	0.03	0.03	0.03	0.04	0.05	0.07
Concrete Bl., painted	0.10	0.05	0.06	0.07	0.09	0.08
Carpet w. pad	0.08	0.24	0.57	0.69	0.71	0.73
Med. velour	0.07	0.31	0.49	0.75	0.70	0.60
Wood floor	0.15	0.11	0.10	0.07	0.06	0.07
Glass	0.18	0.06	0.04	0.03	0.02	0.02
Gypsum brd.	0.29	0.10	0.05	0.04	0.07	0.09
Plywood	0.28	0.22	0.17	0.09	0.10	0.11
Audience(ft ^{2})	0.60	0.74	0.88	0.96	0.93	0.85
upholstered seats (no aud.)	0.49	0.66	0.80	0.88	0.82	0.70

1. That which is from construction materials and air inside the room.

2. That which is intentionally applied to surfaces.

3. That which comes from room furnishings, carpet and audience.

Air absorption is related to distance between the source and listener. Any absorption due to volume will have an effect on high frequencies above 2 kHz. There is a strong relationship between good hearing and good sightlines. In most halls, seats that have poor sight lines also have defective acoustics. Sound whose frequencies are above 1000 Hz (e.g. violin tones) do not bend around corners or obstructions. Remember that the wavelength of sound at 20 Hz is 56.5 feet and at 20 kHz it is 0.0565 ft (5/8 inch).

Reverberation time differs with the frequency coefficient of absorption. A greater value for this coefficient means more absorption. Carpet, velour, audience and empty seats are very absorbent relative to brick, glass and gypsum board. Exactly how much more is indicated in the preceding chart which lists absorption coefficient values at various frequencies for each square foot of a selected material.

Carpets serve the dual purpose of floor covering and noise reduction. Noise reduction is achieved in two ways, carpets absorb the sound energy and movement on carpets produces less noise than on bare floors.

1. Carpets laid directly on bare concrete have a noise reduction coefficient.

2. Fiber type has no influence on sound absorption.

3. Noise reduction increases as pile weight and pile heights increased. Cut pile has greater absorption than loop.

14. Acoustics

4. Pad material has a significant effect.

Normally walls are considered to be sound barriers and the applications of absorbent materials to the walls of a room aid in the reductin of noise levels in a noisy space. While almost any absorption material may be used with success on walls, there is a certain class of material called wall facing or treatment specifically designed for this purpose. These generally have a fiberglass or mineral fiber core covered with fabric. They may be attached directly to the wall or attached by a system of furring strips to create an air gap between the treatment and the wall. As in the case of ceilings, this air gap would serve to decrease the low frequency absorption of the treatment.

Amplification

A general rule is that well designed rooms smaller than 25,000 ft^3 (e.g. 20'wide x 50'long x 25'high) will rarely need amplification. Halls larger than 250,000 ft^3 (e.g. 100'w x 100'l x 25'h) will always require amplification. Rooms in between these dimensions may or may not need amplification depending on other factors.

The need for amplification in rooms for speech is determined by:

1. The amount and quality of background noise

2. The level of the direct speech signal combined with the early reflections

3. The level of the late reflections

4. The difficulty of the message to the listeners

5. The age of the listeners. Older listeners generally have a limited sensitivity to certain frequencies.

Another problem is too much amplification. Small proscenium theatres are often used for big-band or rock concerts that were probably never imagined by the building's designer. When the sound pressure level gets ridiculously high and the building begins to shake, it is well past the time to reduce gain. If the sound level remains high, the best advice is to purchase a set of industrial ear plugs, preferably ones that will reduce the loudness by at least 20 dB.

15. Intercom and Paging

Among the many technical elements of production, invariably the one that receives the least attention prior to the dress rehearsal is backstage communication. However, none of the scene shifts, lighting or sound cues would be able to take place were it not for the ability of the stage manager to give an audible cue. The actors would remain in the green room without hearing the command "places" or being able to hear the progress of the show through a monitor speaker. Yet such an important aspect of the theatre is often taken for granted or left until the last minute for the sound or lighting technician to set up.

Production Communication

One of the ways in which cues were given before the advent of electricity was by means of whistles. Certain patterns of whistling would initiate a variety of scenic transformations. Among the myths of the theatre is that whistling in the playhouse is bad luck. It is easy to see how this superstition derived. Imagine the confusion that would result if a false whistle triggered a complex series of wing, border and machine action.

In order to communicate effectively in the theatre of today, prior planning must take into account the needs of creative and support personnel during rehearsals and performance. The different types of communication required during technical rehearsals are:

1. The stage manager must sit in the house and communicate with the director, designers, running crew and follow spot operators to set cues

2. The lighting designer must sit in the house and communicate with the master electrician in the booth or backstage and follow spot operators in lighting positions to set light cues

147

3. The sound designer must sit in the house and communicate with the sound operator to set levels for sound cues.

During the actual performance the needs are for:

1. Cues and warnings from the stage manager to the running crews, master electrician, sound operator and fly operators

2. Acknowlegement and status reports from the crew back to the stage manager

3. Coordination between the stage manager and house manager for curtain and intermission

4. Cues and warnings from the stage manager to the actors

5. Monitoring action on stage, in the booths and in the dressing rooms so that the stage manager, crew and actors can hear the progress of the performance.

All of the functions listed above, except the last, may be accomplished by a well-designed intercom system. The live monitoring may be accomplished with a dedicated PA system. Both types of systems should be installed in a reasonably equipped theatre. These should have the capability of operating independent of the main sound reinforcement and playback system, but may be capable of interconnecting with the main system in order to hear program information.

Layout

Figure 38 shows a typical layout of intercom stations for a university theatre. The location, purpose, and type of each station is as follows:

15. Intercom and Paging

1. **Dressing rooms.** A wardrobe person or assistant stage manager working with actors will be able to keep in contact with the stage manager. Headset and/or speaker station.

2. **Upstage right.** Running Crew uses this for cueing. Headset station with belt-pack.

3. **Upstage left.** Running crew uses this for cueing. Headset station with belt-pack.

4. **Grid or load floor.** For loading weights or rigging. Headset and speaker station. When loading weights a hands-free station is needed. If a running crew member is up on the grid, as might be required to gently float leaves on cue in the final

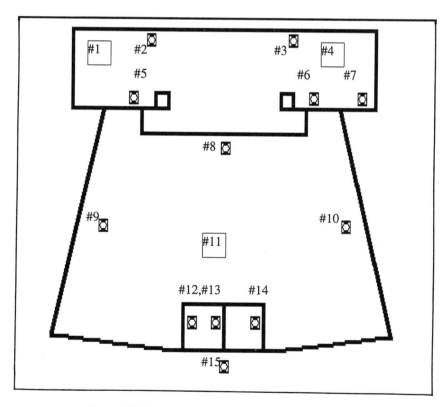

Figure 38. Intercom stations – University Theatre

scene of *Cyrano de Bergerac*, a headset is required to minimize noise during the show.

5. **Downstage right.** Running crew or assistant stage manager uses this for cueing. Headset station.

6. **Downstage left.** Running crew or assistant stage manager uses this for cueing. Headset station.

7. **Fly rail.** Fly crew uses this for cueing. Headset station with multiple outlets.

8. **Orchestra pit.** Conductor in a musical will use this for cueing. Headset station.

9. **Lighting position.** Follow spot operator will use this for cueing. Headset station.

10. **Lighting position.** Follow spot operator will use this for cueing. Headest station.

11. **House position.** Stage manager and designers use this during technical rehearsal. Headset station with multiple outlets.

12. **Control booth.** Stage manager uses this or backstage station to call the show. Headset station.

13. **Control booth.** Master electrician uses this for cueing. Headset station.

14. **Sound booth.** Sound operator uses this for cueing. Headset station.

15. **House control.** House manager uses this to communicate with the stage manager. Telephone handset station.

When specifying a system for installation, the number of stations and the number of channels must be considered. A

15. Intercom and Paging

simple system may have only two channels, A and B. In a two channel system most cues would be called on the "A" channel and cues for special effects or follow spots could be on the "B" channel. More versatile systems will have multiple channels. Four channel systems with A, B, C, and D are common.

Other choices for each station are whether it has an internal speaker, requires a belt pack or can be used with a headset directly connected to the wall station itself. The advantage in having an internal speaker is that "hands-free" operation is possible. The disadvantage is that the audience may be able to hear the cues and that is unacceptable. Internal speakers should only be used in locations away from the audience's hearing range, like in a dressing room apart from the stage. The advantage of a belt pack is that the technician may be mobile while having control over switching, muting, and signaling other stations. The only advantage of a wall station that can be used without a belt pack is that it only requires a headset for operation. Belt packs can get misplaced easily. If the theatre is equipped with stations that will not work without a belt pack, your ability to communicate may be limited if belt packs are lost or misplaced. Both belt packs and wall stations usually have a call light to signal the operator when the headset is removed.

Clear-Com

Starting as a small garage operation in the late 1960s, Bob Cohen and some friends were engaged in building and renting a sound reinforcement system for rock groups in San Francisco. Prior to one show, the promoter requested an intercom system to communicate with the spotlight operators. The result was beginning of the Clear-Com Intercom System.

Clear-Com was established in 1970 and is a recognized leader in the manufacture of high-quality, closed-circuit intercom systems. The system is connected via microphone cables to provide a reliable, versatile and private system. Unlike telephone systems which have a narrow bandwidth, Clear-

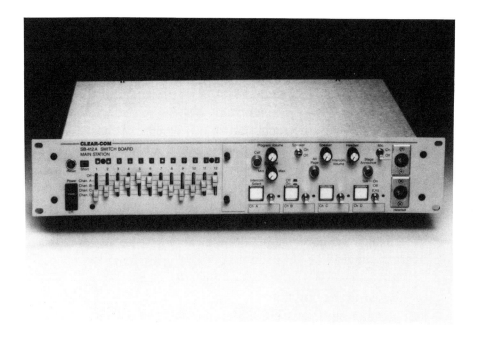

Figure 39. Clear–Com main station with switch board

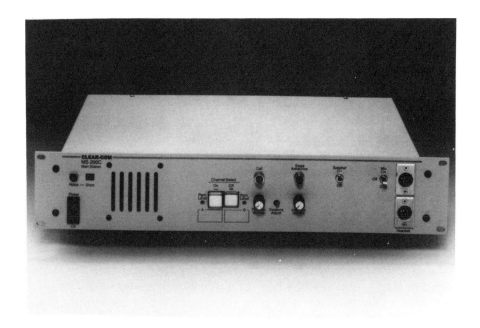

Figure 40. Clear–Com main station with A–B channels

15. Intercom and Paging

Com's main function is to convey clear speech at all volumes and under all conditions.

Clear-Com is a distributed amplifier system: each intercom station contains its own mic preamplifier, power amplifier for headset or speaker, and signaling circuitry. The system does not rely upon a central amplifier. The method of connecting an audio line to an input is via bridging with high impedance. A Clear-Com station's input impedance is about 100 times the impedance of the line connected to that station, so it draws very little audio power. Line levels never drop, even if intercoms join or leave a system. If one station stops working, the

Figure 41. Double-muff headset (Courtesy Clear-Com)

rest of the system continues operating normally. All stations are compatible.

The maximum number of stations with a 2-amp power supply is 100 with no signaling, 50 with signaling, or 20 stations with speakers. The maximum end-to-end distance is 5000 ft. over #22 wire. The power supply is 30 VDC regulated.

The impedance of the dynamic headset is between 300 and 1000 ohms, the microphone is between 150 and 250 ohms. The headsets on FB (program interrupt) systems allow on-air talent to monitor program audio and receive cues from video directors and other production personnel.

The "call" function lets a station operator attract the attention of other operators who have removed their headsets or turned off their speakers. Pressing a station's call button turns on the lamps at stations on the same channel. "Call" also activates remote paging. The remote paging function lets remote stations be designated for announcement via their built-in speakers.

Sidetone adjustment allows the operators to set their own voice level as heard in the headset/speaker system. Sidetone adjustment never affects incoming or outgoing signals.

Paging

Although paging of dressing rooms and other areas may be done through a production intercom system with a combination of headset and built-in speakers, a better solution is to install a separate system dedicated exclusively for that purpose. A 70-volt system is ideal for this purpose (see Chapter 4). In such a system speakers can be switched in and out with no deterioration of the signal. The stage manager may then page the dressing rooms without breaking the attention of the production crew. Pre-show house announcements concerning cast changes or photograph policy can be made through speakers mounted permanently in the house without interfering with the main production speaker system. Finally, the action on stage may be monitored and sent to the dressing rooms, production booths or lobby for latecomers to hear until they can be seated.

A permanent paging system may also be used for a lecture or symposium. It is relatively easy to plug microphones into a permanent system, turn on mixer, amp and speakers, set levels, and satisfy the requirements of lecturer, panelists and audience. The Shure M267 is a compact four channel mixer designed for professional applications. It features four switchable microphone or line-level balanced inputs with individual gain controls and low-frequency roll off switches. The output is switchable for line and microphone level or as an additional unbalanced line feed to drive a tape recorder or power amplifier. It also has simplex power (phantom power) for condenser microphones. A front-panel headphone level control and monitor jack is available for headphones. The unit may be stacked with others to increase the number of channels. Placed in a rack together with an amplifier that has a 70-volt output and an array of permanently mounted speakers, a system can be assembled that will satisfy most of the the paging and monitoring needs in a theatre.

It must be emphasized that a key aspect of such a system is the permanently wired speaker array. A constant-voltage, line-matching transformer designed to match the speaker with a 70-volt line must be used for each speaker. A number of speakers mounted in the wall and ceiling of production areas, green room, dressing rooms and audience, offer an efficient and flexible solution to paging requirements.

Appendix A: Wire Connectors

The most vulnerable parts of the sound hookup are the lengths of cable and the connectors. Among the problems that may occur are internal wire breakage, faulty connectors and cold solder connections. A few guidelines:

1. Do not elbow wrap the cables.

2. Do not disconnect cables by pulling connectors.

3. Check for continuity periodically using a VOM or cable tester especially designed for that purpose (see page 25).

When selecting cable, consider the distance, the gauge, and the amount of wear the cable will take. The length of cable for a given wire size can be doubled if twice the power loss can be tolerated. The next smaller gauge can be used if twice the power loss can be tolerated and the length remains the same.

The chart below may be used for constant voltage systems.

Maximum Length of Cable Run (ft. & m)											
Wire Size	Low Impedance 10% Power Loss						High Impedance 5% Power Loss				
(AWG)	4 Ohm		8 Ohm		16 Ohm		100 Ohm		250 Ohm		500 Ohm	
	ft	m	ft	m	ft	m	ft	m	ft	m	ft	m
14	88	27	176	54	352	101	1045	319	2610	796	5220	1591
16	55	17	110	34	220	67	630	192	1574	430	3150	960
18	35	11	70	21	140	43	410	125	1020	311	2050	825
20	22	7	44	13	88	27	262	80	655	200	1310	399
22	13	4	26	8	52	16	164	49	410	125	820	250
24	8	2	16	5	32	10	105	32	262	80	525	160

Figure 42. Maximum length of cable run by size and impedance

The choice of appropriate audio cables for runs of varying distances depends on many factors, such as amplifier voltage output and power level as well as load impedance and the percent of power loss which can be tolerated. For this reason it is not practical to provide a general chart showing the recommended wire size for all conditions. The chart shows the maximum recommended cable runs for various wire sizes selected for commonly encountered load impedances.

The XLR Connector

The best connector to use for microphone input, line input and line output is an XLR type. Refer to Figure 28 and follow the procedures below.

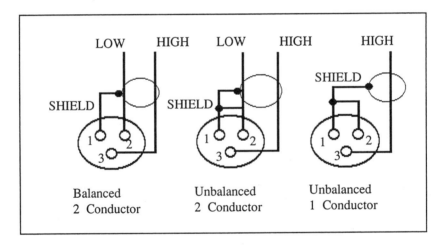

Figure 43. Input/Output XLR wiring

For balanced inputs, wire the XLR connector as follows:

1. Connect the signal leads of a two-conductor shielded cable to pin 3 (high) and pin 2 (low) of the connector.

2. Connect the cable shield to pin 1.

Appendix A: Wire Connectors

For unbalanced inputs using two-conductor shielded cable, wire the XLR connector as follows:

1. Connect the signal leads of a cable to pin 3 (high) and pin 2 (low) of the connector.

2. Connect the cable shield to pin 1 of the connector.

3. Connect a jumper from pin 1 to pin 2 of the connector.

For unbalanced inputs using single-conductor shielded cable, wire the XLR as follows:

1. Connect the center conductor of the single-conductor shielded cable to pin 3 of the connector.

2. Connect the cable shield to pins 1 and 2.

The MIDI Connector

The MIDI cable is a standard 5-pin DIN connector. As shown in the diagram below pin #4 is designated for the signal plus and pin #5 carries the signal minus. Pin #2, at the center of the 5-pin configuration, is used for ground-to-shield. Pins #1 and #3 are not required in the MIDI specification, but may be used for sync pulses. When MIDI devices are connected, "out" plugs into "in" and "in" plugs into "out." A thru

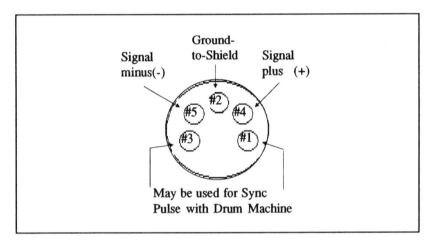

Figure 44. MIDI plug wiring

jack transmits information identical to whatever arrived at the in jack. "Thru" plugs into "in." A MIDI cable carries data in only one direction.

MIDI is not a piece of hardware. It is a communications protocol agreed upon by the MIDI Manufacturers Association (MMA) and the Japan MIDI Standards Committee (JMSC). MIDI data is digital. Information is provided to a receiving device that understands MIDI. It is not an audio signal in the

sense that the MIDI signal itself is audible. The sound in-
itiated by a MIDI event depends entirely upon how the receiving device interprets the MIDI command. The MIDI
specifications are applied by each manufacturer in different
ways. Although basic connections for MIDI devices are the
same, different functions may be controlled by the same channel. A manufacturer who abides by the specifications only
agrees not to send anything out of the MIDI output jack that
does not conform to the protocol.

Practicum

Courtesy of Bob Heil, *Practical Guide for Concert Sound*

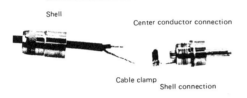

Shell

Center conductor connection

Cable clamp

Shell connection

WIRING AN RCA-TYPE PIN PLUG*

Parts identification and cable preparation.

Strip approximately 1/2″ of outer insulation. Unwrap or unbraid the shield and form a lead. Strip approximately 5/16″ of insulation from the center conductor. Tin both leads.

Solder the shield to the outer surface of the shell connection, allowing enough free shield to wrap the cable around to the center of the connector. Cool the connection immediately with pliers.

Insert the center conductor in the hollow pin, and fill that end with solder. Cool the connection immediately with pliers. Clean any solder splashes and inspect for burned insulation. Pinch the clamp around the outer insulation with pliers, firmly, but not so tight as to cut the insulation.

Slide the shell forward and screw it tightly to the threaded plug.

*Switchcraft No. 3502 connector illustrated. Many large diameter cables are more easily wired to "simple" RCA type pin plugs without a shell (Switchcraft No. 3501M, or equivalent). The braid can then be soldered directly to the shell of the plug.

Appendix A: Wire Connectors

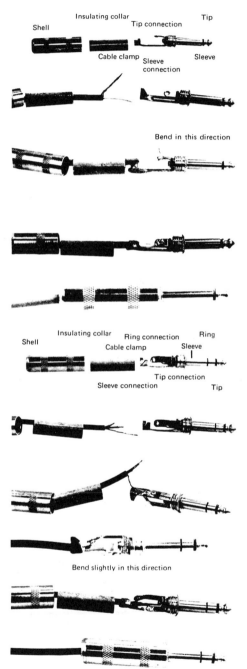

Insulating collar **Tip connection** **Tip**

Shell

Cable clamp **Sleeve connection** **Sleeve**

Bend in this direction

Insulating collar **Ring connection** **Ring**

Shell **Cable clamp** **Sleeve**

Sleeve connection **Tip connection** **Tip**

Bend slightly in this direction

WIRING A STANDARD PHONE PLUG (2-conductor)

Parts identification.

Slide shell, then insulating collar over cable end. Strip outer insulation for length equal to length of sleeve connection. Unwrap or unbraid shield, twist to form lead.

Position outer insulation just ahead of cable clamp, strip center conductor from point just behind tip connection. Tin center conductor and shield. Bend shield as illustrated, solder to outer surface of sleeve connection. (Cool immediately with pliers.) Insert center conductor in tip connection, solder, cut end flush. Bend the end of the tip connector (slightly) toward the sleeve connection to help prevent the burr (from the cut wire) from cutting through the insulating collar.

Using pliers, bend cable clamp around outer insulation. Clamp should be firm, but not so tight as to cut insulation.

Slide insulating collar forward, until flush with rear of threads. Slide shell forward, screw tight to plug assembly.

WIRING A TIP, RING & SLEEVE PHONE PLUG (3-conductor)

Parts identification.

Slide shell and insulating collar over cable end. Strip outer insulation for length equal to length of sleeve connection. Remove any tracer cords and strain relief cords. Form lead from shield. Hold cable with outer insulation just ahead of cable clamp, and strip the red (or white) conductor just behind the tip connection. Then strip the black conductor just behind the ring connection. Tin all leads, and cut the center conductors so approximately 1/8" of bare wire remains.

Solder the shield to the outer surface of the sleeve connection, allowing enough free shield to bend around to the other side of the cable clamp. Cool the connection immediately with pliers.

Insert the center conductor leads in their respective connection points, and solder in place. Trim the leads flush. Bend the end of the tip connection (slightly) toward the ring connection to help prevent the burr (from the cut wire) from cutting through the insulating collar.

Using pliers, bend the cable clamp around the outer insulation. The clamp should be firm, but not so tight as to cut the insulation.

Slide the insulating collar forward, until flush with rear of threads. Slide the shell forward, and screw tightly onto plug.

Sound for the Stage

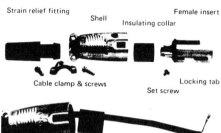

Strain relief fitting | Shell | Insulating collar | Female insert
Cable clamp & screws | Set screw | Locking tab

WIRING A FEMALE XLR CONNECTOR

Parts identification (as the connector is usually packaged).

Insert strain relief in rear of shell. Then slip shell onto cable end, followed by insulating collar. Strip outer insulation approximately 9/16''. (No. 8451 cable illustrated here)

Pull off foil wrap. Strip approximately 5/16'' of insulation from the center conductors, leaving approximately 1/4'' of insulation between the bare wire and the outer insulation. Tin the center conductors, and trim so that about 1/8'' bare wire remains. Then tin the shield conductor, orienting it with the center conductors so they are aligned with the proper pins of the insert. Cut the end of the shield so that it extends 1/16'' beyond the center conductors.

Solder the center conductors to their respective pins, using just enough solder to fill the end of the pin. Yamaha's wiring standard dictates that the black lead mates with pin 3, the white (or red) lead with 2 (see footnote on page 10 of this section). Then solder the shield to pin 1. Clean off any solder splashes, and inspect for burned insulation. Insert the locking tab in the female insert, as illustrated, with small nib facing front of connector.

Slide insulating collar foward, up to rear edge of female insert. The outer insulation of the cable must be flush with, or covered by the end of the insert. If any of the center conductors are visible, the cable clamp may not be able to grip the cable firmly, and the connector leads will soon fatigue. Then slide the collar back into the shell.

Slide the shell forward, orienting the notch in the shell with the locking tab in the insert. Secure the insert in the shell with the set screw. Place the cable clamp over the rear of the shell, with careful attention to the clamp's orientation; a raised lip inside the clamp should be aligned immediately over a lip in the shell for thinner cables (No. 8451). For heavier cables (No. 8412), the clamp should be turned around to offset the lips and provide more clearance for the cable. Insert the clamp screws and tighten fully.

Appendix B: Microphone Chart

This is a list of a few representative microphones used in typical stage applications. It is meant to provide performance guidelines for specifying a microphone of a particular type. A variety of dynamic, condenser and other microphones should be tried before purchasing any brand.

AKG D 321

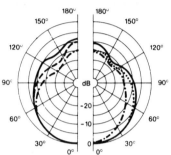

Specifications:
Transducer principle: dynamic pressure gradient microphone
Polar pattern: hypercardioid
Frequency range: 40–20,000 Hz
Electrical impedance at 1,000 Hz: 300 ohms
Maximum SPL: 128 dB

Figure 45. Polar patttern, AKG D 321

Dimensions: length=7.3", max. diameter=1.9"
Included accessories: stand adapter

Shure SM 58

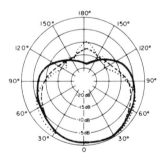

Specifications:
Transducer principle: dynamic pressure gradient microphone
Polar pattern: Cardioid; rotationally symmetrical about microphone axis, uniform with frequency
Frequency range: 50–15,000 Hz
Nominal impedance: 150 ohms
Dimensions: length=6.4", max. diameter=2"

Figure 46. Polar pattern, Shure SM 58

Included accessories: stand adapter

Electro-voice RE 15

Specifications:
Transducer principle: dynamic pressure gradient microphone
Polar pattern: supercardioid
Frequency range: 80–15,000 Hz
Nominal impedance: 150 ohms
Dimensions: length=6.6",
    diameter=1.4"
Included accessories: stand adapter

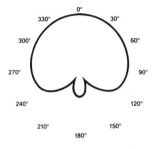

Figure 47. Polar pattern,
E-V RE 15

Sony ECM-55S/55B

Specifications:
Transducer principle: electret condenser microphone
Polar pattern: omnidirectional
Frequency range: 30–18,000 Hz
Electrical impedance at 1,000 Hz: 100 ohms
Dimensions: length=0.84", max. diameter=0.5"
Dimensions, power pack: length=5.25", diameter=0.75"
Included accessories: carrying case, holder clip, wind screen

C-Ducer

Specifications:
Transducer principle: piezoelectric vibration
Tape length available: 60,200 mm
Frequency response (with pre-amp): 3 dB at 25 Hz
and 50 kHz
Included accessories: pre-amp with 1/4" jack output
at 5 k ohms

Appendix B: Microphone Chart

Crown PCC-160

Specifications:
Transducer principle: phase–coherent electret condenser
Polar pattern: half supercardioid
Frequency response: 50 to 18,000 Hz at
30 degrees incidence
Impedance: 150 ohms
Dimensions: length=6.7", width=3.2"

Electro-Voice CL42S

Specifications:
Type: condenser shotgun system
Transducer principle: electret condenser
Polar pattern: hypercardioid
Impedance: 250 ohms
Dimensions: length=16.4", diameter=1.06"

Electro-Voice PL77AA

Specifications:
Type: Single-D condenser cardioid
Transducer principle: electret
condenser
Impedance: 150 ohms
Frequency range: 50–20,000 Hz
Dimensions: length=7.5"
diameter=2" maximum

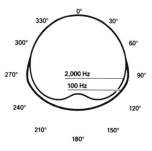

Figure 48. Polar pattern,
E-VPL77AA

167

Appendix C: Product Directory

Amplifiers

Yamaha Corporation
6600 Orangethorpe Ave.
Buena Park, CA 90622
714-522-9011

QSC Audio Products, Inc.
1926 Placentia Ave.
Costa Mesa, CA 92627
714-645-2540

BGW Systems, Inc.
13130 South Yukon Ave.
Hawthorne, CA 90250
213-973-8090

Crown International, Inc.
1718 Mishawaka Rd.
Elkhart, IN 46517
219-294-8000

Crest Audio
150 Florence Ave.
Hawthorne, NJ 07506
201-423-1300

McIntosh Laboratory, Inc.
2 Chambers St.
Binghamton, NY 13903
607-723-3512

Carver Corporation
19210 33rd Ave. West
P.O. Box 1237
Lynnwood, WA 98036
206-775-1202

Microphones

Cetec Vega
9900 Baldwin Place
El Monte, CA 91731
800-877-1771

HM Electronics (HME)
6675 Mesa Ridge Rd.
San Diego, CA 92121
619-535-6060

AKG Acoustics
77 Selleck St.
Stamford, CT 06902
203-348-2121

Shure Brothers, Inc.
222 Hartrey Ave.
Evanston, IL 60202
312-866-2200

C-Tape Developments, Inc.
P.O. Box 1069
Palatine, IL 60078
312-359-9240

Electro Voice
600 Cecil St.
Buchanan, MI 49107
616-695-6831

Telex Communications, Inc.
9600 Aldrich Ave. South
Minneapolis, MN 55420
612-887-5550

Atlas-Soundolier (Mic stands)
1859 Intertech Dr.
St. Louis, MO 63026
314-349-3110

Sony Corporation of America
Sony Drive
Park Ridge, NJ 07656
201-930-1000

Beyer Dynamic
5-05 Burns Ave.
Hicksville, NY 11801
516-935-8000

George Neumann, GMBH
Gotham Audio (U.S. Dist.)
741 Washington St.
New York, NY 10014
212-765-3410

Sennheiser Electronic Corp.
10 West 37th St.
New York, NY 10018
212-239-0190

Paso Sound Products, Inc.
14 First St.
Pelham, NY 10803
914-738-4800

Audio-Technica, U.S., Inc.
1221 Commerce Dr.
Stow, OH 44224
216-686-2600

Loudspeakers

Klipsch
P.O. Box 688
Hope, AZ 71801
501-777-6751

Meyer Sound Labs
2832 San Pablo Ave.
Berkeley, CA 94702
415-486-1166

JBL Incorporated
8500 Balboa Blvd.
P.O. Box 2200
Northridge, CA 91329
818-893-8411

TOA Electronics, Inc.
480 Carlton Ct.
San Francisco, CA 94080
415-588-2538

Polk Audio
1915 Annapolis Rd.
Baltimore, MD 21230
301-358-3600

Bose Corporation
The Mountain
Framingham, MA 01701
617-879-7330

Appendix C: Product Directory

Eastern Acoustic Works
59 Fountain St. Box 11
Framingham, MA 01701
617-620-1478

Altec Lansing
P.O. Box 26105
Oklahoma City, OK 73126
405-324-5311

Turbosound, Inc.
611 Broadway
New York, NY 10012
212-460-9940

Mixing Consoles

Studiomaster Inc.
1340-G Dynamics St.
Anaheim, CA 92806
714-524-2227

Soundcraft
8500 Balboa
Northridge, CA 91329
818-893-4351

Yamaha
(see listing under Amplifiers)

Hill Audio
5002 N. Royal Atlanta Dr. #B
Tucker, GA 30084
404-934-1851

Tascam, Professional Division
of TEAC
7733 Telegraph Rd.
Montebello, CA 90604
213-726-0303

Solid State Logic (SSL)
320 West 46th St.
New York, NY 10036
212-315-1111

AMEK
10815 Burbank Blvd.
North Hollywood, CA 91601
818-508-9788

Tape Recorders

Otari Corp.
2 Davis Dr.
Belmont, CA 94002
415-592-8311

Akai America, Ltd.
2139 E. Del Amo Blvd.
Compton, CA 90220
213-537-3880

Ampex(see listing under Recording Tape)

Tascam
(see listing under Mixing Consoles)

Panasonic Company
Division of Matsushita
Electric Corportation
1 Panasonic Way
Secaucus, NJ 07094
201-348-7000

Studer-Revox America, Inc.
1425 Elm Hill Pike
Nashville, TN 37210
615-254-5651

Tandberg of America
1 Labriola Ct.
Armonk, NY 19594
914-273-6516

Recording Tape

Ampex
Magnetic Tape Division
401 Broadway
Redwood City, CA 94063
415-367-3809

BASF Systems Corporation
Crosby Dr.
Bedford, MA 01730
617-271-4000

Scotch/3M
Magnetic Products Division
3M Center
St. Paul, MN 55144
612-733-1110

Maxell Corporation of
America
60 Oxford Dr.
Moonachie, NJ 07074
201-794-5900

Edit All
X-Edit Corporation
133 South Terrace Ave.
Mount Vernon, NY 10550
914-668-0388

TDK Electronics Corp.
12 Harbor Park Dr.
Port Washington, NY 11050
516-625-0100

Appendix C: Product Directory

Noise Reduction and Signal Processing

Renkus-Heinz
17191 Armstrong Ave.
Irvine, CA 92714
714-250-0166

Dolby Laboratories, Inc.
100 Potrero Ave.
San Francisco, CA 94103
415-558-0200

Industrial Research Products
321 Bond St.
Elk Grove Village, IL 60007
800-255-6993

dbx Inc.
71 Chapel St.
Newton, MA 02195
800-525-7000

Denon America, Inc.
27 Law Dr.
Fairfield, NJ 07006
201-575-7810

Klark Teknik Electronics, Inc.
30 B Banfi Plaza North
Farmingdale, NY 11735
516-249-3660

White Instruments
P.O. Box 696
Austin, TX 78767
512-892-0752

Audio Logic
5639 So. Riley Lane
Salt Lake City, UT 84107
801-268-8400

Wire and Cable

Connectronics Corp.
652 Glenbrook Rd.
Stamford, CT 06906
800-322-2537

Conquest Sound, Inc.
7319 Duvan Dr. Box 757
Tinley Park, IL 60477
800-323-7671

Belden Electronic Wire and Cable
P.O. Box 1980
Richmond, IN 47375
317-983-5200

Wireworks Corp.
380 Hillside Ave.
Hillside, NJ 07205
201-686-7400

Whirlwind Music Dist., Inc.
P.O. Box 1075
Rochester, NY 14603
716-663-8820

West Penn Wire
2833 West Chestnut St.
Washington, PA 15301
800-245-4964

Rental and Purchase

Boynton Studio
Box 130
Morris, NY 13808
607-263-5695

Full Compass Systems
6729 Seybold Rd.
Madison, WI 53719
800-356-5844

Sound Effects

BBC Sound Effects Library
P.O. Box 2053
Princeton, NJ 08543
800-257-5126

Sound Ideas
86 McGill St.
Toronto, Ontario
Canada M5B 1H2
416-977-0512
US 800-387-3030

FirstCom Digiffects
13747 Montfort Dr. Suite 220
Dallas, TX 75240
214-934-2222

Thomas J. Valentino, Inc.
151 West 46th St.
New York, NY 10036
800-223-6278

Intercom

Technical Projects, Inc.
P.O. Box 1449
Barrington, IL 60011
1-800-562-5872

Telex Communications, Inc.
9600 Aldrich Avenue South
Minneapolis, MN 55420
612-884-4051

Clear-Com
945 Camelia St.
Berkeley, CA 94710-1484
415-527-6666

Appendix D: Music Chronology

This chronology is meant to be a guide for those seeking a rudimentary understanding of musical history. Often a production will require a certain period or musical style. Sound Design has only recently been considered a separate design element. In the early part of the twentieth century, Sound Design was accomplished by the Props Master. A review of the opening for the Chicago Little Theatre in October, 1913 concludes:

"Beyond a low, dim hedge looms a rude, red Sunset. Silhouetted against this raw but beautiful Sunset a piping Pan takes a long, melodious Pull at his Pipe. The sound, while remote, is that of a Flute accompanied by a Full Orchestra. Perhaps the Property Man did not know of the orchestra and its fullness when he ordered the Record."

The Middle Ages

590 Church music, Gregorian chants

1000 Troubadours, secular songs in vernacular

1291 Philippe de Vitry, French *Ars Nova*

1346 Guillaume de Machaut, French *Ars Nova*

1364 Francesco Landino, organist and composer

The Renaissance

1420 Guillaume Dufay, *Mass in Three Parts*

1500 Diversification of instruments: clavichord, virginal, spinet, harpsichord, violin and lute

1550 *Book of Common Prayer*, Protestant hymn book

1588 English composer William Byrd publishes madrigals

1597 *Sacrae Symphoniae*, religious music by Gabrieli

Sound for the Stage

17th Century

1607 Monteverdi's opera *Orfeo*; first "modern" orchestra with more than 36 instruments

1674 Giovanni Battista Lully, founder of French opera, directs *Alceste*

1690 Invention of the clarinet

18th Century

1710 Bartolomeo Cristofori develops modern pianoforte in which hammers strike the strings

1712 Antonio Vivaldi composes the twelve concertos known as *Estro Armonico*

1713 Handel writes *Te Deum* and *Jubilate* to celebrate the Peace of Utrecht

1714 Corelli composes *Concerti Grossi*

1721 Bach composes the six *Brandenburg Concertos*

1727 John Gay's *The Beggar's Opera*

1729 Bach's *The Passion According to Saint Matthew* is performed on Good Friday

1740 First public performance of the English anthem "God Save the King"

1741 Handel completes *The Messiah*

Appendix D: Music Chronology

1786 Mozart composes *The Marriage of Figaro*,
subsequently completes *Don Giovanni*,
Così fan tutte, The Magic Flute,
the *E Flat, G Minor* and
C, also known as *The Jupiter Symphony*

1792 French national anthem, "Le Marseillaise"

19th Century

1804 Beethoven composes *Eroica Symphony*

1808 Beethoven's *Fifth Symphony*

1822 Schubert's *Symphony No. 8 in B Minor*, called
the *Unfinished Symphony*

1824 Beethoven's *Ninth Symphony*

1826 Mendelssohn, *A Midsummer Night's Dream Overture*

1830 Hector Berlioz, *Symphonie fantastique*

1831 Chopin settles in Paris

1840 Robert Schumann writes *Dichterliebe*, songs to
poetry by Heine

1844 Berloiz publishes *Treatise on Modern Instrumentation and Orchestration*, which becomes standard
work on symphony orchestras

1848 Stephen Foster writes American folk-music
"Oh! Susanna"

1853 Franz Liszt composes *Sonata in B Minor*, finest
composition for the piano in the romantic era

1867 Johann Strauss, the younger, *The Blue Danube Waltz*
     Moussorgsky's *Night on Bald Mountain*

1874 Strauss, *Die Fledermaus*

1876 Richard Wagner, *Der Ring des Nibelungen*
     Tchaikovsky composes music for *Swan Lake*
     Edvard Grieg writes *Peer Gynt Suites*
     Brahms scores *C Minor* (1876), *D Major* (1877)
     F Major (1883) and *E Minor* (1885)

1878 Gilbert and Sullivan, *H.M.S. Pinafore*

1884 Rimsky-Korsakov composes *Scheherazade*

1889 Cesar Franck, *Symphony in D Minor*

1893 Antonin Dvorak, *Fifth Symphony From the New World*

1894 Claude Debussy, impressionist school of music,
     L'Après midi d'une Faun

1896 Strauss, *Also Sprach Zarathustra*

20th Century

1900 Sibelius' *Finlandia*

1902 Gustav Mahler, *Third Symphony*

1910 Gabriel Fauré's piano composition *Nine Preludes*
     Igor Stravinsky, *Firebird*

1912 Maurice Ravel's *Daphne et Chloé Suite*

1919 Manuel de Falla's *The Three-Cornered-Hat* ballet

Appendix D: Music Chronology

1924 George Gershwin's *Rhapsody in Blue*
Arthur Schoenberg, *Suite for Piano*
Respighi's *Pines of Rome*

1925 Duke Ellington organizes his first band
Aaron Copland's *Symphony for Organ and Orchestra*

1928 Ravel's *Bolero*

1935 Gershwin's *Porgy and Bess*

1936 Sergei Prokofiev's music for *Peter and the Wolf*

1937 Dimitri Shostakovich, *Fifth Symphony*
Béla Bartók's *Music for String Instruments, Percussion and Celestra*

1939 Charles Ives' *Second Piano Sonata* performed
(written between 1904 and 1915)

1943 Rodgers and Hammerstein's *Oklahoma!*

1944 Aaron Copland's *Appalachian Spring*

1956 Karlheinz Stockhausen creates an electronic
music composition, *Gesang der Junglinge*

1958 Pierre Boulez writes *Improvisation sur Mellarme*

1962 United States tour of the Beatles

1969 Woodstock
John Cage, *HPSCHD*

1972 Leonard Bernstein's *Mass* opens JFK Center

1977 Robert Wilson, *Einstein on the Beach*

1985 Concerts for Live Aid, London and Philadelphia

Appendix E: Cue Sheets

The cue sheet should be organized in such a way that it is clear and easy to read. The section below from *The Hostage* is used as an example to illustrate where the cues occur in the script. An excerpt from the cue sheet follows.

SOLDIER [*to the audience*]. Well, that's got rid of her. Now the thing is will Teresa go to the cops? Even if old Einstein is half sozzled there's still the other two to get through. Will they shoot me? Yeah, I s'pose so. Will Teresa go to the cops? No.

QA

There is an explosion which shakes the house and smoke wreathes the stage. Sirens blow, whistles scream and all the lights go out. PAT *and* MEG *rush into the room and they and the soldier hide behind the table. Pandemonium breaks out. What is actually happening is that* MULLEADY *has informed on* PAT *and* MONSEWER *and has brought the police to rescue* LESLIE. *He has involved* RIO RITA *and* PRINCESS GRACE *in his schemes and they have corrupted his morals. The* RUSSIAN *has been a police spy all along. The police are now attacking the house and* MULLEADY *and* RIO RITA *are guiding them in.*

PAT. Take cover, there's a raid on.

MEG. I want to see what's going on.

PAT. Get your head down. They'll open fire any minute.

MULLEADY [*from the roof*]. Stand by. Two of you stay on the roof. The rest come down through the attic with me.

RIO RITA [*from the cellar*]. Six round the front, six round the back. The rest come down through the attic with me.

QB

PAT. And take your partners for the eightsome reel. [*The piano plays.*]

MULLEADY. O'Shaunessy!

O'SHAUNESSY [*from the rear of the house*]. Sir!

MULLEADY. O'Shaunessy, shine a light for Jesus' sake.

O'SHAUNESSY [*off*]. I will, sir.

MULLEADY. Shine a light, I can't see a bloody thing.

O'SHAUNESSY [*off*]. I can't, sir, the battery's gone.

MULLEADY. To hell with the battery.

QC

RIO RITA. Charge!

QD

His party go charging across the stage, but don't know where they're going or what they're doing. After confusion, they all charge back again.

QE

MULLEADY [*off*]. Right, down you go, O'Shaunessy.

O'SHAUNESSY. After you, sir.

MULLEADY. After you, man.

O'SHAUNESSY. After you, sir; I'm terrified of heights.

MULLEADY. Then close your eyes, man. This is war.

QF

Pandemonium as the battle intensifies. Whistles and sirens blow, drums beat, bombs explode, bugles sound the attack, bullets ricochet and a confusion of orders are shouted all over the place. Bodies hurtle from one side of the stage to the other and, in the midst of all the chaos, the kilted figure of MONSEWER *slow marches, serene and stately, across the stage, playing on his bagpipes a lament for the boy in Belfast Jail.* PAT *screams at him in vain.*

PAT. Sir! Sir! Get your head down. Get down, sir—
there's a raid on. [*He touches* MONSEWER.]

MONSEWER. What? [*He stops playing and the din sub-sides.*]

PAT. There's a raid on.

MONSEWER. Then why the devil didn't you tell me?
Man the barricades. Get the Mills bombs. Don't fire, lad-die, till you see the whites of their eyes.

QG

SOLDIER. I've only got a bottle.

MONSEWER. Up the Republic!

PAT. Get your head down, sir; they'll blow it off.

RIO RITA [*from under the stairs*]. Pat, do you want to buy
a rifle?

PAT. Get out will you? [RIO RITA *goes.*]

*The din subsides and the battle dies down. Inside the room
are* MONSEWER, *in command,* PAT *by the window, and*
MEG, COLETTE, ROPEEN *and* LESLIE *crawling
round on the floor. Around the room the shadowy shapes of
the forces of law and order flit in and out, darting across the
stage and under the stairs.*

From *Behan, The Complete Plays*,
©Copyright 1978, Grove Press, New York

Sound Cue Sheet

Production: <u>The Hostage</u>

Cue #	Location	Source	Duration	Input	Output	Action	Notes
A 1	Act III	CD	3 sec	m1,m2 @7	s1,s2 @9	play CD	explosion
2	p129	Tape A	3 min	m3,m4 @7	s3,s4 @6	play tape	sirens, chaos
B	p129	Tape B	8 sec	m1,m2 @7	s7 @6	play tape	piano
C	p130	CD	3 sec	m1,m2 @8	s1 @9	play CD	explosion SR only
D	p130	CD	3 sec	m1,m2 @8	s2 @9	play CD	explosion SL only
E	p130	Tape B	12 sec	m5,m6 @6	s1,s2 @5	play tape	glass breaks, dogs, shouts
F	p130	Tape A	15 sec	m3,m4 @7	s1,s2 @5	play tape	bullets,drums & whistles
G	p131	CD	3 sec	m1,m2 @8	s1,s2 @9	play CD	explosion

Note: "m" stands for mixer input channel
"s" stands for speaker output channel

Appendix F: Bibliography

Aiken, James, "Digital Sampling Keyboards," *Keyboard,* December 1985.

Ballou, Glen, Editor-in-Chief, *Handbook for Sound Engineers: The New Audio Cyclopedia,* 1987.

Bartlett, Bruce, *Introduction to Professional Recording Techniques,* Howard W. Sams & Co., Indianapolis, IN, 1987.

Bellman, Willard, *Scene Design, Stage Lighting, Sound, Costume and Makeup,* Harper and Row, New York, 1983.

Beranek, Leo L., *Music, Acoustics and Architecture,* John Wiley and Sons, New York, 1966.

Brook, Rollins, *Fundamentals of Sound in the Theatre,* Bolt, Beranek & Newman, Canoga Park, CA, 1980.

Burris-Meyer, H. and Mallory, V., *Sound in the Theatre,* Theatre Arts Books, New York, 1959.

Collison, David, *Stage Sound,* Cassell, London, England, 1982.

Heil, Robert, *Practical Guide for Concert Sound,* Volume 2, Melco Publishing, Marissa, IL, 1985.

Izenour, George C., *Theatre Design,* McGraw-Hill, New York, 1977.

Moog, Robert, "The Keyboard Explosion," *Keyboard,* October, 1985.

National Institute for Occupational Safety and Health, *Compendium of Materials for Noise Control,* May, 1980.

Simonson, Lee, *The Stage is Set,* Theatre Arts Books, New York, 1963.

Small, Richard H., "Closed-Box Loudspeaker Systems," *Journal of the Audio Engineering Society,* Volume 20, December 10, 1972.

Theile, A. N., "Loudspeakers in Vented Boxes," *Journal of the Audio Engineering Society,* Volume 19, May 5, 1971.

Wood, Alexander, *The Physics of Music,* Barnes & Noble, New York, 1964.

Appendix G: Glossary of Terms

acoustic suspension - a type of loudspeaker which uses a closed-box.

acoustic coupling - connecting loudspeaker drivers together to achieve greater gain. The principle is also used in the Bose 901 loudspeaker with identical drivers hooked in series. "Coupled" this way they cannot all resonate at the same frequency; therefore the drivers divide into different frequencies to reproduce sound.

alnico magnet - a magnet made from aluminum and nickel alloy used in loudspeaker drivers.

amplifier - a device which enables an input signal to control power from a source independent of the signal. Thus, it is capable of delivering an output which bears some relationship to, and is generally greater than, the input signal.

anechoic chamber - a room in which reflected sound is practically eliminated. Used for measuring the characteristics of loudspeakers and microphones.

attack - how fast gain changes after threshold has been exceeded.

attenuator (loss pad) - an electronic device inserted between microphone and preamplifier which, through resistance, eliminates input overload by lowering microphone output.

audiophile - an individual who seeks perfection in the recording and reproduction of sound. The discriminating listener can be considered in this category, but the fanatic is known to spend large sums of money in pursuit of the ideal.

auxiliary - an additional output path assignment in a mixer which allows the connection of external devices either pre- or post-fader, or the set up of several independent mixes for different musicians. These can be grouped via a bus network or used individually for each input module, depending on the design of the mixing console.

azimuth adjustment - the adjustment to position the head gap exactly perpendicular to the horizontal base of the tape.

baffle - the panel to which most speakers are mounted, usually the front panel of an enclosure.

balanced input - interconnectors utilize two conductors plus a ground, usually to the cable shield. Three pins are necessary with balanced inputs. Also known as low level, 600 ohm, Lo-Z or microphone input. However, this type of connection is used for more than just microphones.

bandwidth - the audio frequency range. In digitally sampled sound, bandwidth is determined by sampling rate.

bass reflex - a type of speaker enclosure that has an opening which permits rear sound waves to emerge in phase with sound from the front.

beam splitter - a partial mirror that allows a laser beam to pass through in one direction and be reflected back to an optical sensor.

bias - a high-frequency alternating current fed into the recording circuit and used as a carrier of audio signals to the record head, as well as current to the erase head.

bits per sample - numbers are stored in digital memories as groups of binary digits, called bits. Each bit in a sample accounts for a factor of two in the accuracy of a digital number. Thus, if a sample is recorded as an 8-bit number, that means the dynamic range of the input waveform is divided into 256 (two raised to the eighth power) possible levels, one of which is recorded.

boost - increasing the signal level. Often refers to raising the level of bass or treble frequencies during equalization.

bridging - the shunting of one signal circuit by one or more circuits usually for the purpose of deriving one or more circuit branches.

bulk eraser - a strong alternating electromagnetic device used to erase the magnetic patterns on tape while still wound on a reel, or in bulk form.

boundary - any large acoustically hard surface such as a floor, wall or ceiling where the microphone assembly is placed.

capstan - the rotating shaft which engages the tape and pulls it across the heads at constant speed.

carbon microphone - one of the earliest types of microphones still in use today primarily in telephones. Consists of carbon granules in a brass cup attached to center of a metallic diaphragm. Requires DC power to operate.

cardioid - microphone with a heart-shaped polar response, making it most sensitive in one direction.

Appendix G: Glossary of Terms

compressor - a transducer which, for a given input amplitude range, produces a smaller output range. Also a variable gain amplifier which has a fixed gain that doesn't affect output level until the input level exceeds a given dynamic threshold.

condenser microphone - a microphone which has a diaphragm consisting of a movable plate of a condenser (capacitor). When polarized by applying a direct current voltage, motion of the diaphragm in relation to a fixed backplate produces an output voltage.

cone - diaphragm of a conventional moving coil loudspeaker.

CPS - cycles per second.

cross talk - signal leakage between two channels.

crossover network - in multiple loudspeaker systems, a circuit employing electrical filters of frequency-discriminating paths for routing high, low and middle frequencies to the particular speakers designed to handle them.

cut - decreasing the signal level. Often used to describe reducing bass or treble levels during equalization.

damping (of a loudspeaker) - expresses the ability of the cone to stop moving as soon as the electrical input signal ceases. Poor damping allows motion to continue briefly like an automobile with poor shock absorbers. This hangover creates a "booming" sound in the bass frequencies masking clarity.

damping factor - ratio of loudspeaker impedance to amplifier source impedance. A large ratio improves loudspeaker damping.

DAT - digital audio tape. Recording tape that uses sampling and digital data to store sound. Also refers to the player.

decibel (dB) - a relative measure of sound intensity. One dB is the smallest change in sound volume that the human ear can detect. Also used to express logarithmically voltage and power ratios.

degaussing - the process of demagnetizing tape recorder heads and metal parts of the tape transport mechanism.

delay - an effect commonly used in contemporary recordings which produces independently variable left and right channel signal delays. The result is a "doubled" sound.

demagnetizer - a device for removing magnetic force fields from tape heads and metal parts of the tape transport mechanism.

diaphragm - sound generating element of a loudspeaker.

DIN - abbreviation for for *Deutsche Industrie Norm*, a West German standard for equalization and connection.

directional characteristics - ability to respond to different sound waves in relation to their incoming location.

distortion - any difference between the original sound and the recorded and reproduced sound.

distortion, harmonic - nonlinear distortion of a system or transducer characterized by the appearance in the output of harmonics other than the fundamental component when the input wave is sinusoidal.

distortion, intermodulation - nonlinear distortion of a system or transducer characterized by the appearance in the output of frequencies equal to the sums and differences of integral multiples of the two or more component frequencies present in the input wave.

Doppler effect - the change in pitch of a sound heard by an observer when the sound source is in motion. It is called the Doppler effect after an Austrian, Christian Johann Doppler (1803-53), who first explained it.

dubbing - the act of duplicating on tape.

dynamic microphone - an electromagnetic type which employs a moving coil in a magnetic field.

dynamic range - the ratio between the overload level and the minimum acceptable signal level in a system or transducer.

echo - a wave which has been reflected or otherwise returned with sufficient magnitude and delay to be perceived in some manner as a wave distinct from that directly transmitted.

editing - selecting certain sections of tape recordings, deleting unwanted portions and splicing them together in the desired sequence.

Appendix G: Glossary of Terms

effects - altering the sound signal with electronic or LSI (large scale integration) technology to create natural reverberation, echo, delay, flanging, pitch changes or other effects.

EIA - abbreviation for Electronics Industries Association, a standards organization for microphone sensitivity and connection.

electronic crossover - a method of dividing frequencies sent to loudspeakers using an electronic circuit.

equalization - the manipulation of frequencies that are required to meet the recognized standards of recording and reproducing techniques.

erase head - the magnetic assembly on tape recorder over which the tape passes to remove previously recorded signals.

fader - a potentiometer that controls the loudness of a signal.

feed reel - the reel on a tape recorder which supplies the tape.

feedback - a howl produced in a sound system that occurs when the output of the loudspeaker enters the microphone or guitar pickup and is reamplified.

flange effect - combination of delay and low frequency oscillation modulation. It can dramatically thicken the sound of keyboards or produce the aircraft sound popular among guitarists. The resultant variations in pitch and stereo imaging are known as "flanging."

flat response - any audio system is specified as having an essentially flat frequency response if it is rated plus or minus 3 dB from 50 to 15,000 Hz.

Fletcher-Munson curve - a sensitivity curve plotted for the human ear showing its characteristic for different intensity levels between the threshold of hearing and the threshold of feeling. These data are often referred to as equal loudness contours.

flutter - very short and rapid variations in tape speed.

frequency - the rate of repetition in cycles per second of musical pitch, as well as of electrical signals. Low frequencies refer to bass tone, high frequencies to treble tone.

frequency response - the manner in which the output of a device responds to and varies with changes in input frequency.

A "flat response" microphone, for example, indicates near-equal response over the entire range of frequencies. In obtaining optimum performance, frequency response is often "tailored" by introducing low-frequency "roll off" and controlled high-frequency "boost." These roll offs and boosts must be accomplished smoothly and abrupt variations in the frequency response curve indicate poor microphone quality.

frequency spectrum analysis - using a real-time analyzer to see the various frequencies that are present in a particular sound.

gain - the increase in signal provided by an amplifier between input level and output level.

graphic equalizer - a particular type of equalizer which operates simultaneously on a relatively large number of frequency bands. May adjust 27 bands 1/3 octave wide or 11 bands almost an octave wide. Each band has its own slider control for boost and cut. These controls are arranged on the front panel in order of increasing frequency horizontally left to right, and increasing gain vertically, thereby giving a graphic representation of the chosen frequency response.

ground - a point in any electrical system that has zero voltage, usually the chassis of any electrical component.

Haas effect - as the first sound to be heard takes command of the ear, any sound arriving up to 50 milliseconds later seems to arrive as a part of and from the same directions as the original sound. This restores intelligibility and eliminates confusion.

head - an electromagnetic device across which the tape is drawn and which magnetizes the coating of the tape.

head alignment - in tape recorders, the correct position of the tape head and gap, with respect to the magnetic tape.

headroom - the difference between peak and average system level, usually about 10 dB.

Hertz (Hz) - a unit measuring frequency; equals one cycle per second.

horns - compression drivers mounted in metal, fiberglass or plastic enclosures for high-frequency reproduction.

Appendix G: Glossary of Terms

hum - low-frequency noise in an audio component usually induced from the power line or stray magnetic or electrostatic fields.

impedance - a common characteristic of electrical devices expressed in ohms. It is the AC resistance of any electrical system. Generally referred to as either "high" or "low" impedance. Microphones are classified as either high Z (10,000 ohms and up) or low Z (50 ohms to 250 ohms). Low-Z microphones permit the use of longer cables without high-frequency roll off. For best results in connecting two components, output and input impedances must match.

information surface - the surface of a laser disc, usually aluminum or tellurium, on which pits are read using a laser diode to code sound signals as digital data. A high power laser is used to burn the pits into a master glass surface in the manufacturing process.

input - the receptacle or jack through which a signal is fed into an amplifier.

IPS - abbreviation for tape speed in inches per second.

jack - receptacle or plug connector leading to the input or output circuit of a tape recorder or other component.

laser diode - a solid state laser used in compact disc players to detect pits and reflective surfaces.

lavalier microphone - a microphone designed to be worn around the neck or attached by a clip to the clothing.

LED - light emitting diode. Used as an indicator light.

level indicator - indicates the level at which the recording is being made and serves as a warning against under or over recording. It may be in the form of LED indicators or a VU meter.

line level - also known as unbalanced level. Inputs are high impedance, usually around 10 k ohms.

mains - refers to main electric power feed for equipment, or to the primary loudspeakers used for output from a mixer via amplifiers.

micron - one millionth of a meter. Pits in the information surface of a compact disc are 0.1 microns deep.

microphone - a transducer which converts sound into an electrical output or voltage.

MIDI - musical instrument digital interface. A standard to connect electronic instruments to controllers and each other.

mil - 1/1000 of an inch. Tape thickness is usually measured in mils.

mixer - a device by which signals from two or more sources can be combined and fed simultaneously into a tape recorder at the proper level and balance.

monitor - checking signals during a recording or playback by listening on a separate loudspeaker or by watching a level meter.

NAB curve - standard playback equalization curve set by the National Association of Broadcasters.

Nyquist frequency - refers to the highest frequency a given device can safely sample.

off-axis - in relation to a microphone or loudspeaker, represents a location that is not on a line perpindicular to the front.

Ohm's law - an equation which expresses the relationship between voltage (E), amperage (I) and resistance (R). It is E=IR.

optical sensor - a device within a compact disc player that reads the reflected pattern of light.

oscillator - a device for producing a continuous electrical oscillation, or pure tone, at any desired frequency. Often oscillators are built into mixers or tape decks to provide a constant signal for checking the throughput (continuity path).

oscilloscope - a device which forms a graphic representation of an electrical signal on a screen (cathode ray tube). Used for testing and measuring of electrical and electronic equipment.

output - the signal voltage coming from components, such as preamplifiers and amplifiers. In tape recorders, there are line outputs, speaker outputs and monitor outputs.

oxide - as used in magnetic tape, a microscopic ferrous oxide.

overload distortion - distortion caused by too great an input signal to an amplifier or preamplifier. This distortion is not controlled by volume setting and most frequently occurs when microphones are used close to the sound source. It is controllable with an attenuator.

pad - a nonadjustable passive network which reduces the power level of a signal without introducing appreciable distortion.

pan pot - a panoramic potentiometer that places a signal across two stereo lines (left and right). It controls the location of the sound between the two extremes of left and right. If the pan pot is placed at the center position, an equal amount of signal will be fed to both sides and the image in the stereo picture will be central.

parametric equalization - requires an equalizer with extreme flexibility, since there are many parameters that can be adjusted, such as frequency, amount of boost and cut, and the bandwidth of the activity.

passive crossover - consists of large coils of wire and huge capacitors inserted between the output of the power amp and speaker. They are designed to cut out the treble to the bass speaker and the bass tones to the treble driver.

patch cord - a short cable with a plug at either end used to interconnect equipment, such as tape recorders and amplifiers.

patch panel - an arrangement of jacks in a rack to which various and inputs are wired. It allows flexibility to connect different inputs and outputs provided impedance matching is maintained.

PFL - prefade listen. This button will solo the signal on the monitors with the feed for this solo taken before the fader.

phantom power - a method of supplying necessary voltage to a condenser or electret microphone without the use of batteries. Typical voltages are between +18VDC and +48VDC. ONLY used with a balanced line. Feeds a DC voltage down the same line. Blocking capacitors keep the DC voltage from straying into the audio sections of the mixer.

phase cancellation - occurs when two similar or identical signals are out of step in time. Waveforms displaced by 180 degrees tend to cancel.

phasing - the polarity orientation of the two speakers used in stereo playback. Also refers to polarity orientation of microphone connectors.

pinch roller - a rubber roller which engages the capstan, pulls the tape with constant speed and prevents slippage.

piston range - the effective excursion range of a driver. Determines the lowest frequencies a driver can produce.

pitch change - to change the tone of an input signal. Digital effects processors can change pitch in semitone increments over a plus/minus one-octave range. Fine adjustment of pitch in one-cent (1/100th of a semitone) increments/decrements is also possible.

playback head - the magnetic head which picks up signals from tape for playback.

plug - a form of mechanical interconnector used for quick and easy connection of components, such as phone plug, phono plug and AC plug.

polar pattern - response graph of microphone sensitivity through a 360-degree axis.

polarity - refers to the positive and negative direction of electricity or magnetism.

pop filter - an acoustically transparent shield placed above the microphone diaphragm, often wrapped around the exterior of the microphone, which sharply reduces the bad effects of explosive vocal sounds but does not affect desired microphone performance.

pop sensitivity - the measure of a microphone's reaction to explosive vocal sounds, like "P," "T," and "F." A microphone with high pop sensitivity will create a very disturbing low-frequency "boom" in the sound system. Microphone types vary widely in their pop sensitivity.

potentiometer - a variable resistor used for volume and tone controls.

power amplifier - an amplifier designed to operate a speaker system.

power cord - cable used to connect a component to AC current.

preamplifier - an amplifier that boosts extremely weak signal voltages, such as those from microphones, magnetic playback heads or phonograph pickups, to a level that is usable by power amplifiers, and at the same time accomplishes the necessary equalization for industry standards.

print through - when tapes are stored for long periods of time in a tightly wrapped configuration the magnetism can be exchanged; thus, signals recorded can transfer to adjacent pieces of tape, resulting in mixed sounds when the tape is played back.

psychoacoustics - the interaction of human perception and architectural/mechanical characteristics of environment.

release - how fast gain returns to unity after input signal falls below threshold.

resonant frequency - the tendency of any physical body to vibrate most freely at one particular frequency as a result of excitation by a sound of that particular frequency.

reverberation - the persistence of sound within a space after the source of that sound has ceased.

RIAA equalization - an equalizer is used to reduce the lows and boost the highs when all master recordings are cut; otherwise, the stylus that cuts the master would vibrate out of its groove when a full deep bass tone was fed to it. The RIAA (Recording Institute Association of America) curve becomes audible only if it is uncorrected by the manufacturer of your preamp, amplifier and speakers.

signal-to-noise ratio - the ratio, measured in dBs, between the pure sound and the noise induced by the recording system itself.

simul-sync - technique of recording sound on sound by mixing a recording from one track with a subsequent recording on another track. During this process, the record head is used as a playback head to synchronize the sound.

slate - routes the control room microphone signal to all the buses in a mixer for announcing on tape the name of the recording or take number. In some consoles, a low-frequency tone is put on the tape during slating so that the beginning of the take can be quickly located by listening for tape tones during fast forward or rewind.

slew rate - the speed at which a transistor tracks a rapidly changing input signal. Slewing rate is expressed in volts-per-microsecond. A slew rate of 32 volts/microsecond means that a transistor is capable of passing a voltage change from 1 to 32 volts in one-millionth of a second.

SMPTE - abbreviation for the Society of Motion Picture and Television Engineers, which developed the time-code for synchronization of recorders.

sound pressure level (SPL) - volume (loudness of sound), expressed as a logarithmic ratio of intensity. The threshold of human hearing at 1000 Hz is approximately 0 dB SPL.

spider - a circular piece of spring-like corrugated fabric used to guide the movement of the voice coil so that it remains centered in the narrow slot of the magnetic assembly.

splicing - joining together of two pieces of tape while editing.

splicing block - a device for holding the two pieces of tape to be spliced while they are being attached.

splicing tape - a special pressure-sensitive nonmagnetic tape used for splicing magnetic tape.

take-up reel - the reel located on the right side of the tape recorder which accumulates the tape as it is recorded or played.

tape guides - grooved metal posts located on either side of the head assembly to keep the tape tracking properly across the heads.

tape index counter - a digital counter used mostly to aid in referring to a particular portion of tape.

tape speed - the speed at which tape moves past the heads, measured in inches per second.

tape splicer - a semiautomatic or automatic device used for splicing tape.

tape transport - the mechanical portion of the tape recorder mounted with motors, reel spindles, heads and controls. It does not include pre-amplifiers, speakers or carrying case.

tension arm - a part of the tape transport mechanism on a tape recorder that keeps the correct tightness on the tape. It may be used as a switch to detect when the tape is no longer present. At the end of the tape, the recorder will switch off automatically.

timbre - the characteristic quality of a musical instrument which permits it to be distinguished from another. Timbre depends on the harmonic or overtone structure of the instrument.

time-code - a 1200-Hz square-wave signal used to synchronize tape machines.

transducer - device for converting from one form of energy to another, e.g., a microphone converting from acoustical to electrical, a loudspeaker driver from electrical to acoustical.

transistor - a semiconductor device, invented by Dr. William Shockley, Dr. John Barden, and Dr. Walter H. Brattain of the Bell Telephone Laboratories in 1948. The name "transistor" is coined from two words, transfer and resistor. The first transistor consisted of a particle of semiconductor material, such as germanium, mounted in a holder with two point contacts.

turntable - a device, soon to be a relic, which spins a vinyl record at a constant speed using a belt- or direct-driven motor. It must also have a tonearm and cartridge to pickup the sounds out of the record grooves.

tweeter - a driver designed to reproduce only the high frequencies of the audible spectrum.

unbalanced input - interconnections that utilize one conductor while the shield is used for the other conductor and ground. Only two pins are necessary with unbalanced input, also known as high level, Hi-Z or line level input.

vented box - a loudspeaker enclosure that has an open port to the outside permitting sound waves to emerge in phase.

voice coil - the metal coil of a moving coil loudspeaker.

VOM - volt ohm meter. Used to test continuity and voltage.

VU meter - a voltmeter calibrated in volume units which indicates the relative levels of audio signals and is used to set recording levels.

woofer - a low frequency cone driver.

working distance - the distance from the performer or instrument to the microphone.

wow - repetitive slow variations in tape speed.

Index

Index

Index

About the author: Patrick M. Finelli is Associate Professor at the University of South Florida lecturing in sound design, lighting, computer technology and theatre history. His experience spans a wide variety of stage and arena productions, including drama, dance, opera, symphony, jazz, summer stock, television, film and political debates. He was born in Boston and educated at the University of California at Berkeley where he is completing requirements for the Ph.D. degree. Editor and principal author of USITT's *Directory of Software*, he has also written a screenplay about Gordon Craig, Isadora Duncan and the Art Theatre.

LIBRARY
ST. LOUIS COMMUNITY COLLEGE
AT FLORISSANT VALLEY

LIBRARY
ST. LOUIS COMMUNITY COLLEGE
AT FLORISSANT VALLEY.